# THE
# CAHUILLA

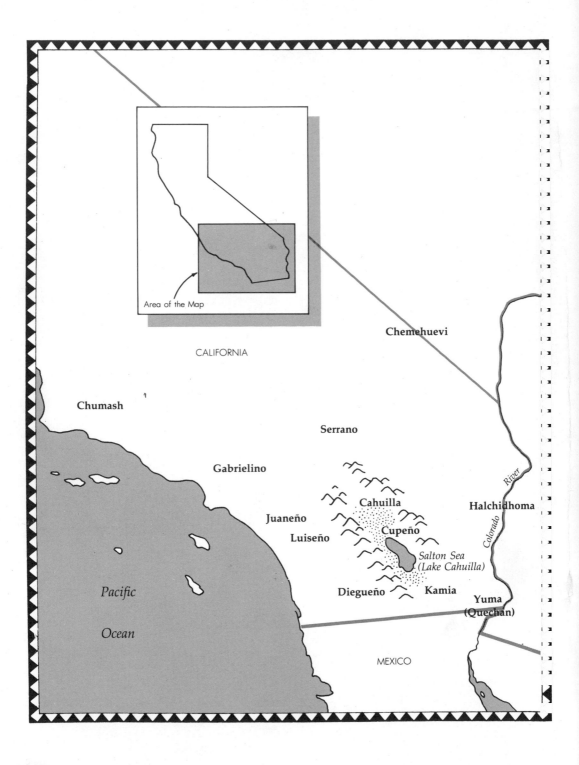

Area of the Map

CALIFORNIA

Chemehuevi

Chumash

Serrano

Gabrielino

Cahuilla

Juaneño

Cupeño

Luiseño

Halchidhoma

Salton Sea
(Lake Cahuilla)

Pacific

Diegueño          Kamia

Yuma
(Quechan)

Ocean

Colorado River

MEXICO

INDIANS OF NORTH AMERICA

# THE
# CAHUILLA

*Lowell John Bean*
*California State University at Hayward*

*Lisa J. Bourgeault*
*Southwest Museum*

Frank W. Porter III
*General Editor*

CHELSEA HOUSE PUBLISHERS
*New York   Philadelphia*

*On the cover* Jar-shaped basket, 11½ inches high.

**Chelsea House Publishers**
*Editor-in-Chief*  Nancy Toff
*Executive Editor*  Remmel T. Nunn
*Managing Editor*  Karyn Gullen Browne
*Copy Chief*  Juliann Barbato
*Picture Editor*  Adrian G. Allen
*Art Director*  Maria Epes
*Manufacturing Manager*  Gerald Levine

**Indians of North America**
*Senior Editor*  Marjorie P. K. Weiser

*Staff for* **THE CAHUILLA**
*Deputy Copy Chief*  Ellen Scordato
*Editorial Assistants*  Tara P. Deal, Clark Morgan
*Assistant Art Director*  Laurie Jewell
*Assistant Designer*  Donna Sinisgalli
*Picture Researcher*  Alan Gottlieb
*Production Coordinator*  Joseph Romano

First Printing

1  3  5  7  9  8  6  4  2

Library of Congress Cataloging in Publication Data

Bean, Lowell John.
The Cahuilla.
(Indians of North America)
Bibliography: p.
Includes index.
Summary: Examines the culture, history, and changing
fortunes of the Cahuilla Indians.
1. Cahuilla Indians. [1. Cahuilla Indians. 2. Indians of North
America—California] I. Bourgeault, Lisa J.   II. Title.
III. Series: Indians of North America (Chelsea House
Publishers)
E99.B39   1989      306'.08997                 88-16187

ISBN 1-55546-693-1
     0-7910-0355-8 (pbk.)

# CONTENTS

# INDIANS OF NORTH AMERICA

CHELSEA HOUSE PUBLISHERS

# INDIANS OF NORTH AMERICA: CONFLICT AND SURVIVAL

## Frank W. Porter III

*The Indians survived our open intention of wiping them out, and since the tide turned they have even weathered our good intentions toward them, which can be much more deadly.*

John Steinbeck
*America and Americans*

When Europeans first reached the North American continent, they found hundreds of tribes occupying a vast and rich country. The newcomers quickly recognized the wealth of natural resources. They were not, however, so quick or willing to recognize the spiritual, cultural, and intellectual riches of the people they called Indians.

*The Indians of North America* examines the problems that develop when people with different cultures come together. For American Indians, the consequences of their interaction with non-Indian people have been both productive and tragic. The Europeans believed they had "discovered" a "New World," but their religious bigotry, cultural bias, and materialistic world view kept them from appreciating and understanding the people who lived in it. All too often they attempted to change the way of life of the indigenous people. The Spanish conquistadores wanted the Indians as a source of labor. The Christian missionaries, many of whom were English, viewed them as potential converts. French traders and trappers used the Indians as a means to obtain pelts. As Francis Parkman, the 19th-century historian, stated, "Spanish civilization crushed the Indian; English civilization scorned and neglected him; French civilization embraced and cherished him."

Nearly 500 years later, many people think of American Indians as curious vestiges of a distant past, waging a futile war to survive in a Space Age society. Even today, our understanding of the history and culture of American Indians is too often derived from unsympathetic, culturally biased, and inaccurate reports. The American Indian, described and portrayed in thousands of movies, television programs, books, articles, and government studies, has either been raised to the status of the "noble savage" or disparaged as the "wild Indian" who resisted the westward expansion of the American frontier.

7

Where in this popular view are the real Indians, the human beings and communities whose ancestors can be traced back to ice-age hunters? Where are the creative and indomitable people whose sophisticated technologies used the natural resources to ensure their survival, whose military skill might even have prevented European settlement of North America if not for devastating epidemics and the disruption of the ecology? Where are the men and women who are today diligently struggling to assert their legal rights and express once again the value of their heritage?

The various Indian tribes of North America, like people everywhere, have a history that includes population expansion, adaptation to a range of regional environments, trade across wide networks, internal strife, and warfare. This was the reality. Europeans justified their conquests, however, by creating a mythical image of the New World and its native people. In this myth, the New World was a virgin land, waiting for the Europeans. The arrival of Christopher Columbus ended a timeless primitiveness for the original inhabitants.

Also part of this myth was the debate over the origins of the American Indians. Fantastic and diverse answers were proposed by the early explorers, missionaries, and settlers. Some thought that the Indians were descended from the Ten Lost Tribes of Israel, others that they were descended from inhabitants of the lost continent of Atlantis. One writer suggested that the Indians had reached North America in another Noah's ark.

A later myth, perpetrated by many historians, focused on the relentless persecution during the past five centuries until only a scattering of these "primitive" people remained to be herded onto reservations. This view fails to chronicle the overt and covert ways in which the Indians successfully coped with the intruders.

All of these myths presented one-sided interpretations that ignored the complexity of European and American events and policies. All left serious questions unanswered. What were the origins of the American Indians? Where did they come from? How and when did they get to the New World? What was their life—their culture—really like?

In the late 1800s, anthropologists and archaeologists in the Smithsonian Institution's newly created Bureau of American Ethnology in Washington, D. C., began to study scientifically the history and culture of the Indians of North America. They were motivated by an honest belief that the Indians were on the verge of extinction and that along with them would vanish their languages, religious beliefs, technology, myths, and legends. These men and women went out to visit, study, and record data from as many Indian communities as possible before this information was forever lost.

8

By this time there was a new myth in the national consciousness. American Indians existed as figures in the American past. They had performed a historical mission. They had challenged white settlers who trekked across the continent. Once conquered, however, they were supposed to accept graciously the way of life of their conquerors.

The reality again was different. American Indians resisted both actively and passively. They refused to lose their unique identity, to be assimilated into white society. Many whites viewed the Indians not only as members of a conquered nation but also as "inferior" and "unequal." The rights of the Indians could be expanded, contracted, or modified as the conquerors saw fit. In every generation, white society asked itself what to do with the American Indians. Their answers have resulted in the twists and turns of federal Indian policy.

There were two general approaches. One way was to raise the Indians to a "higher level" by "civilizing" them. Zealous missionaries considered it their Christian duty to elevate the Indian through conversion and scanty education. The other approach was to ignore the Indians until they disappeared under pressure from the ever-expanding white society. The myth of the "vanishing Indian" gave stronger support to the latter option, helping to justify the taking of the Indians' land.

Prior to the end of the 18th century, there was no national policy on Indians simply because the American nation had not yet come into existence. American Indians similarly did not possess a political or social unity with which to confront the various Europeans. They were not homogeneous. Rather, they were loosely formed bands and tribes, speaking nearly 300 languages and thousands of dialects. The collective identity felt by Indians today is a result of their common experiences of defeat and/or mistreatment at the hands of whites.

During the colonial period, the British crown did not have a coordinated policy toward the Indians of North America. Specific tribes (most notably the Iroquois and the Cherokee) became military and political pawns used by both the crown and the individual colonies. The success of the American Revolution brought no immediate change. When the United States acquired new territory from France and Mexico in the early 19th century, the federal government wanted to open this land to settlement by homesteaders. But the Indian tribes that lived on this land had signed treaties with European governments assuring their title to the land. Now the United States assumed legal responsibility for honoring these treaties.

At first, President Thomas Jefferson believed that the Louisiana Purchase contained sufficient land for both the Indians and the white population.

Within a generation, though, it became clear that the Indians would not be allowed to remain. In the 1830s the federal government began to coerce the eastern tribes to sign treaties agreeing to relinquish their ancestral land and move west of the Mississippi River. Whenever these negotiations failed, President Andrew Jackson used the military to remove the Indians. The southeastern tribes, promised food and transportation during their removal to the West, were instead forced to walk the "Trail of Tears." More than 4,000 men, women, and children died during this forced march. The "removal policy" was successful in opening the land to homesteaders, but it created enormous hardships for the Indians.

By 1871 most of the tribes in the United States had signed treaties ceding most or all of their ancestral land in exchange for reservations and welfare. The treaty terms were intended to bind both parties for all time. But in the General Allotment Act of 1887, the federal government changed its policy again. Now the goal was to make tribal members into individual landowners and farmers, encouraging their absorption into white society. This policy was advantageous to whites who were eager to acquire Indian land, but it proved disastrous for the Indians. One hundred thirty-eight million acres of reservation land were subdivided into tracts of 160, 80, or as little as 40 acres, and allotted to tribe members on an individual basis. Land owned in this way was said to have "trust status" and could not be sold. But the surplus land—all Indian land not allotted to individuals— was opened (for sale) to white settlers. Ultimately, more than 90 million acres of land were taken from the Indians by legal and illegal means.

The resulting loss of land was a catastrophe for the Indians. It was necessary to make it illegal for Indians to sell their land to non-Indians. The Indian Reorganization Act of 1934 officially ended the allotment period. Tribes that voted to accept the provisions of this act were reorganized, and an effort was made to purchase land within preexisting reservations to restore an adequate land base.

Ten years later, in 1944, federal Indian policy again shifted. Now the federal government wanted to get out of the "Indian business." In 1953 an act of Congress named specific tribes whose trust status was to be ended "at the earliest possible time." This new law enabled the United States to end unilaterally, whether the Indians wished it or not, the special status that protected the land in Indian tribal reservations. In the 1950s federal Indian policy was to transfer federal responsibility and jurisdiction to state governments, encourage the physical relocation of Indian peoples from reservations to urban areas, and hasten the termination, or extinction, of tribes.

Between 1954 and 1962 Congress passed specific laws authorizing the termination of more than 100 tribal groups. The stated purpose of the termination policy was to ensure the full and complete integration of Indians into American society. However, there is a less benign way to interpret this legislation. Even as termination was being discussed in Congress, 133 separate bills were introduced to permit the transfer of trust land ownership from Indians to non-Indians.

With the Johnson administration in the 1960s the federal government began to reject termination. In the 1970s yet another Indian policy emerged. Known as "self-determination," it favored keeping the protective role of the federal government while increasing tribal participation in, and control of, important areas of local government. In 1983 President Reagan, in a policy statement on Indian affairs, restated the unique "government to government" relationship of the United States with the Indians. However, federal programs since then have moved toward transferring Indian affairs to individual states, which have long desired to gain control of Indian land and resources.

As long as American Indians retain power, land, and resources that are coveted by the states and the federal government, there will continue to be a "clash of cultures," and the issues will be contested in the courts, Congress, the White House, and even in the international human rights community. To give all Americans a greater comprehension of the issues and conflicts involving American Indians today is a major goal of this series. These issues are not easily understood, nor can these conflicts be readily resolved. The study of North American Indian history and culture is a necessary and important step toward that comprehension. All Americans must learn the history of the relations between the Indians and the federal government, recognize the unique legal status of the Indians, and understand the heritage and cultures of the Indians of North America.

Under the Palms—Cahuilla, *a photograph by Edward S. Curtis.*
*Curtis's pictures of the Cahuilla were published in 1926 in volume*
*XV of* The North American Indian, *a 20-volume series that took*
*the photographer more than 30 years to complete.*

# THE
# CAHUILLA
## AND THEIR
# ENVIRONMENT

It looked like rain in the land of the Cahuilla. The people worried that the rain might fall before they had a chance to gather the acorns. If this happened, the acorns would be ruined and food would be scarce. A *puul* (a man with magic powers) from one community recalled a rain song taught to him by his guardian spirit. He held a ceremony to stop the rain, singing the song and rubbing a charmstone for power to help the spiritual beings keep the rain away. He implored the rain to stay away and not destroy the acorns because the people needed food. The people knew that if the puul was sincere in his request, the rain would stay away until the acorns were all gathered.

The Cahuilla Indians lived in an area of about 2,400 square miles in the southern part of what is now California. They used wild animals and plants for their sustenance. Natural disasters such as extreme weather conditions, heavy winds, floods, droughts, fires, and earthquakes could ruin their food supply.

According to archaeologists, the Cahuilla first traveled from the north to their southern California home perhaps 2,000 to 3,000 years ago. The objects that the ancient Cahuillas left behind provide clues about how they lived when they first came to that area. The stone projectile (weapon) points of the earliest Cahuillas indicate that they hunted some of their food. After living for some time in southern California, they learned from their eastern neighbors how to make pottery, which they used for cooking and as storage jars for water and for the plant foods they ate. They also made baskets for food storage. Archaeologists know that the Cahuillas spent time painstakingly collecting small seeds because they used a type of grinding stone generally used to make flour out of grass and other tiny

13

seeds. They made pendants and beads out of sea shells that must have been obtained through trade with people who lived near the coast. Many delicate ornaments of abalone and olivella shell have survived thousands of years of exposure to the desert climate or burial in the earth. The ornaments were probably worn as jewelry and used as money in addition to being given as gifts and used for sacred purposes.

Some Cahuillas lived around a lake that no longer exists—Lake Cahuilla, which was located about where the Salton Sea is today. Remains indicate they ate fish, shellfish, and water plants and birds, as well as land animals and plants from areas close by. When the lake dried up around A.D. 1500, the people relied on the nearby hills and mountains more than before for water, food, and new homes; there they found acorns and many other foods to eat.

The territory of the Cahuilla in southern California has always been in the same general area inhabited by their ancestors as long as 2,000 or 3,000 years ago. It had tall mountains, deep valleys, rocky canyons, passes (low places in the middle of mountain ranges), and arid desert land. The altitude dipped to 273 feet below sea level at the Salton Sink but towered 11,000 feet above sea level in the San Bernardino Mountains. Nowhere was there lush, green growth. Both the mountains and desert land looked barren, but they were actually full of hundreds of resources that helped the Cahuilla live well. These resources included materials such as palm fronds for building houses and a huge variety of plants and animals for food.

*Ravines in the bed of Lake Cahuilla, drawn in 1856 by surveyors seeking a railroad route to the Pacific Ocean. The present-day Salton Sea occupies part of the site of the original lake, which dried up about A.D. 1500.*

*Palm Canyon in southeastern California extends from the valley floor up to 400 feet.*

*Screwbean mesquite, one of the many plants that flourished in the low desert zone, was a source of edible blossoms and seedpods during the summer months. These nutritious foods could be prepared in various ways.*

The plants and animals of the hot, dry desert were different from those found in the colder, wetter mountains. There were four major environmental zones in Cahuilla territory, each at a different level and each containing its own characteristic plants and animals. The people were able to hunt game and gather plants in all four zones without traveling very far, because mountains, valleys, and canyons were distributed evenly through their territory. Over hundreds of years the Cahuilla had discovered which plants and animals in each zone were the best raw materials for making houses, tools, and other objects that they used every day. They knew which provided the best food and how to prepare the food in tasty ways.

Each of the zones was defined by its altitude. The Lower Sonoran Life Zone was a desert. It made up almost two-thirds of Cahuilla territory, starting from the very lowest land up to about 3,500 feet above sea level. The desert could be as hot as 125 degrees Fahrenheit in the summer, and some areas averaged only about 3.5 inches of rain per year. Despite the heat and lack of rain, the low desert zone contained many plants that provided food, such as cacti, palm trees, mesquite, century plant (agave), yucca, screwbean mesquite, catsclaw, desert lily, and several

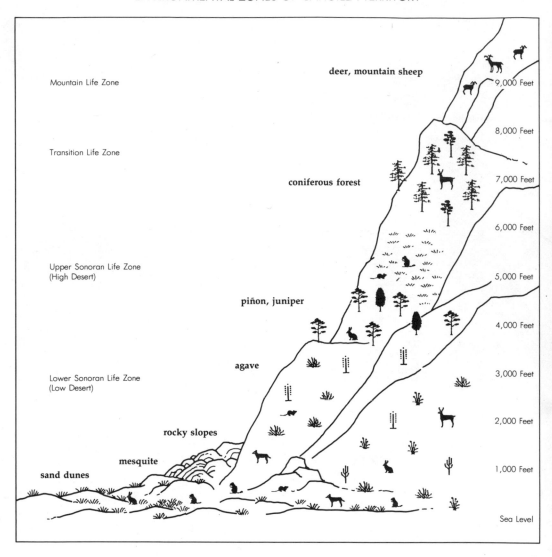

wild fruits. And many creatures, such as antelope, chipmunks, rabbits, mice, rats, deer, reptiles, insects, doves, quail, ducks, and migratory geese, inhabited the area.

The Upper Sonoran Life Zone was a high desert, from 3,500 feet to 6,300 feet above sea level. Here there were the cooler temperatures and moist climate necessary for nut-bearing trees such as piñon (*Pinus monophylla*, a type of pine) and oak trees. Several fruits, such as elderberries, also grew well in the high desert zone. Many of the low desert plants, such as cacti, agave, and yucca, also thrived in the high desert zone. Antelope and rabbits inhabited the high desert in great numbers. The Cahuillas obtained almost two-thirds of their food from the high desert areas in their territory.

Above the desert zones and below the mountain zone was the Transition Life Zone, which extended up to 9,000 feet above sea level. Cooler temperatures and more rain and snow (about 20–30 inches of precipitation per year) allowed forests and meadows to grow in this zone. Oak trees flourished there, along with delicious wild berries. Deer, mountain sheep, squirrels, and desert mice were available in abundance, but hunters had to beware of the dangerous bears and mountain lions that also lived in the transition zone.

The Mountain Life Zone was found in the very highest mountain areas, above 9,000 feet. This region was too cold and snowy for most plant foods to grow, but some game animals lived there in the summer. Cahuilla hunters often went to the mountain zone, where they found deer, mountain sheep, rabbits, squirrels, and smaller animals.

The people needed to get food and other resources from all four zones because the supply from each area was unstable from season to season and from year to year. The amount of rain that fell each year was unpredictable; fires, earthquakes, and strong winds also made the environment uncertain. In years when heavy rains fell, there was plenty of water available in lakes, rivers, wells, springs, and other water sources. Too much rain at a time, however, could cause devastating flash floods that destroyed food resources and even entire communities. But in years when little rain fell, the desert was too dry to support enough plants and animals to feed the people well. Dramatic variations in rainfall could also occur from one environmental zone to the next and in different seasons each year.

The Cahuilla were never surprised by unusual weather and the unpredictable changes in their natural environment. They knew that since the beginning of time, a strong and unpredictable force, or energy, had been a

*From the bottom of a canyon in the low desert zone, the Cahuillas could see all the higher environmental zones of their territory.*

# THE CAHUILLA LANGUAGE

The language spoken by the Cahuillas was related to the languages of the Hopi, Comanche, Luiseño, and Serrano Indians, among others. These all belong to a group of many languages known as the Uto-Aztecan family.

Languages not only have different ways of expressing ideas but they also have different ways of pronouncing and entirely different sounds. The Cahuilla language had some sounds that are not used in English. To pronounce the Cahuilla words in this book, follow these rules:

Any vowel that is doubled has the same sound but is pronounced for twice as long as a single vowel.

Pronounce **a** as in f**a**ther.

Pronounce **e** as in b**e**d.

Pronounce **i** almost like *i* in h**i**t, but with a hint of a long *e* sound as in qu**ee**n.

Pronounce **u** almost like *u* in p**u**sh, but with a hint of a long *u* sound as in June.

The ? indicates a glottal stop; this sounds somewhat like a gulp, or like a *k* sound made far back in the throat.

Pronounce **h** as in **h**ouse.

Pronounce **q** almost like a *k* sound but made slightly farther back in the throat than the English *k* sound.

Pronounce **x** as an *h* sound as in **h**ouse but with more air used to make a harsher sound.

Pronounce **ly** like *li* in mil**li**on.

Pronounce **ng** like *n* in o**n**ion.

All other sounds are pronounced as in English.

part of all things. They called this creative force or power *?iva?a*. (The symbol *?* is used to represent a sound of Cahuilla speech pronounced almost like a gulp.) It was neither good nor bad; it was, however, unpredictable. All the ?iva?a could suddenly leave an area or cause earthquakes, floods, droughts, or other natural disasters. Because ?iva?a could come and go, people could never be certain that the world around them would not change suddenly. Furthermore, people had ?iva?a, although in different degrees, and they could control it. If treated correctly, ?iva?a could be beneficial, but if treated improperly, it could cause serious harm. But some people obtained a great deal of the power at birth or through rituals or gifts from their parents or spiritual guardians. Any person with a lot of power had the great responsibility of using it correctly for everyone's benefit, and especially to ensure enough food for everyone. But some people used their force for evil purposes. They might cause food plants to dry up and die, game animals to disappear from an area, earthquakes, flash floods, and personal misfortune.

Because people and things, including the wind, rain, stars, rocks, animals, and plants, all had ?iva?a, they all interacted in a single system. In fact, Cahuillas did not think of humans as holding a unique place in the world or being rulers of the natural world. Humans, just like everything else, were an integral part of nature and the entire universe. All beings shared in the workings of the universe. Human action could have an effect on other parts of the system. Therefore, humans, like all other beings, had to act responsibly. This responsibility involved protection of other life forms. For example, Cahuillas would not waste the plants they used for food. To be responsible to the universal system, they did not take all the edible parts of a plant or all the seeds. They left something to help the plant grow again.

Like people everywhere, Cahuillas wondered how this whole system had begun and how people, animals, and plants had first appeared on the earth. Their religious leaders explained the beginning of the earth and the Cahuilla people in a literature passed down from generation to generation. Cahuillas did

*A net, or religious leader, photographed in the 1920s. The net had a great deal of ?iva?a (spiritual power) and therefore was responsible for using it wisely.*

not have a system of writing, so they transmitted history orally. The children heard historical, religious, and other stories so often they learned them well and, in turn, would tell them to their children. Thus, even without writing, Cahuilla accounts of the earliest times have come down to us today. One creation story was told in the 1920s by Alejo Patencio, a Cahuilla religious leader who lived in Palm Springs, to the anthropologist William Duncan Strong. Strong wrote it down so that people who speak English could read it. It was considered a sacred and literal account, although abbreviated, of the creation and was a version of their history believed by Cahuillas. In it, ?iva?a, represented by a swirling mass of colors, creates the two first beings who then use ?iva?a to make everything else.

> In the beginning there was nothing but darkness. Red, white, blue, and brown colors all came twisting to one point in the darkness, and they produced two embryos. The children inside grew and talked to one another. They rolled back and forth, and they stretched their arms and knees to make a hole in the sack of colors so they could get out. Then they named themselves Mukat and Temayawut. They made the center pole and earth to form the world, and they made the ocean and water creatures and the sky. Mukat had black mud and Temayawut had white mud to make creatures from, and they each started to make the body of a man. Mukat worked slowly and carefully, modeling a fine body such as men have now. Temayawut worked rapidly, making a rude body with a belly on both sides, eyes on both sides, and hands like the paws of a dog. Temayawut worked three times as fast as Mukat and had a great number of crude bodies finished, compared to the few good bodies made by Mukat. They had a fight about whose bodies were better and how they should live and die, so Temayawut took all his creatures with him and went away.
>
> Then all of Mukat's creatures became alive. The sun suddenly appeared, and all Mukat's creatures were so frightened that they began to chatter like blackbirds, each in a different language. Mukat heard one

man speak the Cahuilla language, and he pressed him to his side and let the others run around. This man was the ancestor of the Cahuilla people and now lives in the abode of the sun, moon, and evening star. Thus only Cahuillas speak the original language.

The early creatures were huge, unlike present-day people or animals. As Francisco Patencio, the brother of Alejo and, like him, a religious leader, explained, "In the first time, when all things were new-made, all creatures and things were very large. The common fly which is about us today was a very large animal." These early beings, called *nukatem*, had much more ?iva?a than any humans, and so they did amazing things, which were known through the stories passed down to each new generation of Cahuillas. Most of the nukatem stopped being active long ago. Over time, they turned into stars, the moon, mirages, rainbows, and other natural objects. When Cahuillas looked at the night sky or a rainbow or body of water, they remembered the early times of the world.

Menily, the moon maiden, was one of the very few female nukatem. A story told by the Patencio brothers describes Menily at the beginning of time and explains how she came to live in the sky.

> Now Menily the moon maiden was a very fine young growing woman, a very beautiful, intelligent young woman, such as all Indian girls have

hoped to be, and she was teaching the people, especially the girls. She took the young people to a place of water, and taught them to dance and run and jump and wrestle and play games, different for the boys and different for the girls. She taught the girls and women to rise and bathe in the pool before the men got up. Then, just as the sun came up, she taught them to shake out their hair backward and forward, to thoroughly untangle it, and then as the sun shone on it, it would never turn gray, nor get blossoms at the ends [split ends]. She taught them how to laugh and be merry.

One night Mukat caused a deep sleep to come upon the people. Then he made trouble to the moon maiden, because she had no one to protect her. When the moon maiden went back to the pool, the place of dancing, she was not happy like herself. She was pale and sick, and thinking that she did not want to stay at that place any more. Her brothers and sisters were asking what was the matter. She did not tell them anything, but she made a song, and then everybody understood what had happened to her.

After that she became quite happy again, and all the people were glad, but they did not know what was going to happen. That night she caused them to sleep deeply. They did not see or hear anything, and that night she went up into the sky. The next morning, all her brothers and sisters could not find her anywhere. There was no track of which way she went. They sent Coyote to look for

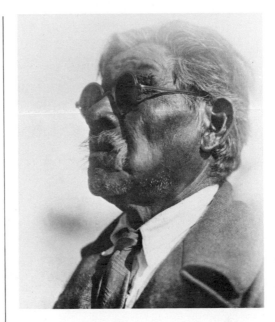

*Alejo Patencio, a Cahuilla religious leader, in a photograph taken in the 1940s.*

her, but he could not find a trace of where she went.

Then one evening, they saw her in the pool, looking up and laughing at them. She was in the sky but they were seeing her in the water. They were so happy to see her again, they all yelled, "Here is our sister in the water," and they all begged her to come out. But she would not come out. They called Coyote. "Our brother, you better come and drink this water, and let our sister come out." Coyote began to drink the water. He could not drink it all, it was too much, but he made it much lower. And yet the moon laughed and did not come up from the pool. Then they looked up and saw her in the sky. This was the first time of the new moon.

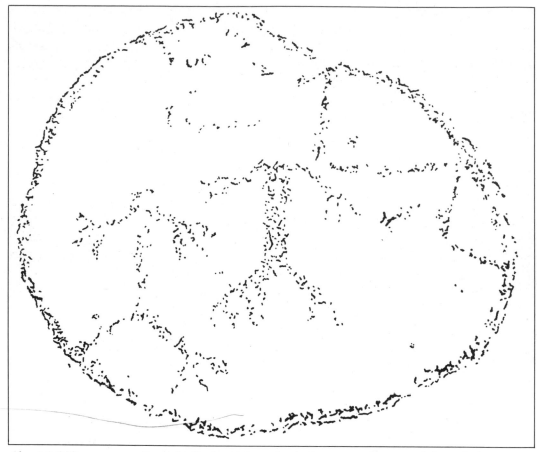

*About 1,000 years ago, the Cahuilla began to make designs on rocks to mark boundaries or, like these, for ritual uses. Rock paintings are in sheltered areas where the colors could not be damaged by the weather. This copy of a pictograph, originally gray, black, white, and yellow, shows two humanlike forms; the angles at right may be mountains.*

There were many nukatem, each with its own name and distinctive personality. Taqwus was a most dramatic nukatem. He sometimes came out in the night and early morning to steal souls and cause other trouble. Usually he could be seen as a meteor or as a humanlike form giving out blue sparks. Kutya?i also worked at night to capture souls. He was usually seen in the form of a whirlwind, and any contact with him was dangerous. Even now, as an older Cahuilla woman recently said, "If whirlwind comes and knocks your clothing from the line, you can't pick it up or wear them or Kutya?i will take your *tewlavil* [soul]." Another of the nukatem was Pemtemweha, the master of hooved animals. He gave hunters permission to kill large game animals, especially deer. In fact, he himself often took the form of a white deer. Muut, the messenger of death, was appointed to his role by Mukat. He often looked like an owl or could be heard in the distance, hooting like an owl.

All the nukatem helped connect the distant past of the first days of the world with the present. Through their physical presence in the form of deer, the moon, whirlwinds, or other natural objects, they helped the Cahuillas to remember and follow the teachings of the stories from the early time.

Through the stories passed down from generation to generation, Cahuillas today still know about the customs and beliefs of their ancestors before their way of life was changed by contact with people from Europe and the United States in the late 18th century. Through the stories they have told to non-Indian friends and scientists, their knowledge of important ceremonies and many details of daily life before the contact period has now been preserved in writing. In the future, Cahuillas and other people, non-Indians as well as Indians, will always have these stories told by their elders. ▲

The Harvester—Cahuilla, *photographed by Edward S. Curtis in 1924.*

# WORKING
## AND
# LIVING WITH OTHERS

By the time Cahuilla children reached adulthood, they already knew how to do most of the tasks required of them; they had started training for their adult roles almost as soon as they could walk. Part of this training was done through games. Certain games were played only by boys—they held tug-of-war contests, wrestled, had pretend battles, practiced target shooting and throwing, and ran races. These games strengthened their muscles and taught them the skills they would need for hunting and warfare. Girls played other games; they juggled, spun tops, made string figures (cat's cradle) using strong plant fibers for string, and played at jackstones (using small rocks). These games helped them develop strong and nimble fingers for making baskets, collecting tiny seeds, grinding acorns, and other daily tasks.

There were a few games that all Cahuillas—men, women, and children—played, such as kickball, shinny, and running races: These games were fun, and they kept people in good physical condition so they would have enough endurance for hunting and gathering. To play shinny, boys and girls stood together in a long line and tried to get a wooden ball between two sticks used as goalposts. First a boy might hit the ball with a curved wooden stick, and then a girl could kick the ball on down the line. At last, working together as a team, they made a goal, as the other side looked on.

Adults also enjoyed games, especially gambling games. Not only did the participants gamble on the outcome of the games, but onlookers would make side bets with each other as well. The stakes would be baskets, tools, or any material items.

The smallest children were allowed to play all day, but older boys and girls worked along with adults. As soon as they were able, they helped their mothers or older brothers and sisters collect plant foods. They also helped the older people during big, communal rabbit hunts. Children spent much of their time with their grandparents, who taught them, partly by telling them stories, how they should act when they became men and women. It was important for children to learn more than food-getting skills; girls had to learn the behaviors and attitudes that were appropriate for women, and boys had to learn the equivalents for men.

By the time they were eight or nine years old, boys were spending less time at play and more with their fathers and grandfathers, learning how to hunt and make tools, and girls were beginning to learn how to prepare food and make baskets under the supervision of their mothers and grandmothers. Girls also prepared for the time when they would have children of their own by helping to care for their younger brothers and sisters.

Another important part of growing up was learning about the food supply and how to make use of it. The Cahuillas' knowledge of all the plants and animals in the area allowed them to live well. They used their knowledge to help schedule their labor, so there were enough people on hand to do the harvesting or hunting tasks necessary. This meant that they were prepared in July to pick mesquite seedpods, in August to pick piñon nuts, and in late October to pick acorns. But some people had to keep hunting, picking wild fruits and berries, and digging up tubers and roots, so they would not run out of these foods. In all seasons, people had to work hard to store up enough food for winter, when they would work on such tasks as making tools and baskets.

One important way of scheduling food-collection activities so that they would all get done was to divide the tasks according to age and sex. Men and women and older and younger people had very different tasks. Young men did most of the strenuous hunting, and older men hunted smaller animals with easier methods. Men of all ages usually did the butchering. Men made the stone, bone, and wooden tools necessary for hunting and cooking; they also made rough baskets. Young women gathered much of the plant food, and older women took care of many of the food preparation tasks. Women made nets, baskets (both rough baskets and finely woven baskets with geometric designs), clothing of animal skins, and clay pots. Depending on their ages, children helped out in whatever way they could.

Almost all the Cahuilla's food came from harvesting plants. Although they did not usually plant these crops, they did practice management of them. They pruned and watered and otherwise cared for important food plants. They supplemented these naturally occurring foods by cultivating small crops of corn, beans, melons, and squash planted in the low desert. They were able to get all the necessary vitamins and other important nutrients by eating a wide variety of nutritious and delicious plants and large and small game animals all year.

The most important part of any Cahuilla food-collection technique was knowledge of the environment. They had to know which plants were edible only when ripe and at what time of year each would ripen. They had to know what plants they could substitute in their diets if cold weather ruined some other food they usually ate. They also had to know about the habits of all the game animals, including when and where to find them and how to catch them. They had to know how to get the food and other supplies they needed from all four of the different environmental zones in their territory. Getting all of this food took a lot of hard work. Men, women, and children had important jobs to do each day in order to provide and prepare enough food for everyone. People's daily tasks and the foods they ate varied with the time of year and the plants and animals available in each zone. There were more than 200 edible plants and more than 100 types of animal food sources in their various environments.

Acorns were a staple of their diets, one of the foods most often eaten and relied on at all times. Acorns, the seeds of oak trees, which flourished in the high desert and transition zones, ripened in October or November, depending on weather conditions. To be certain of a good harvest, Cahuillas monitored the oak groves each year so

*A Cahuilla woman demonstrates the patterns that can be formed from string looped over the wrists and fingers and passed back and forth between the two hands. Making string figures is known in English as "cat's cradle," from the shape of one common pattern. Among the Cahuilla it is a children's pastime and is also used by adults to predict the sex of an unborn child.*

they could start picking as soon as the acorns became ripe. If the groves were very far from their homes, the people camped there for several days or a week or two.

Immediately after a three-day harvest ceremony, everybody worked together to pick and prepare the acorns. Some men or young boys would climb

*Acorns were a staple of the Cahuilla diet. They were gathered in the fall (left) and husked (center), then either ground into flour or stored for later use.*

up in the trees and shake the branches so the acorns would fall to the ground, while others hunted deer and other animals in the area. The women and children remained on the ground to pick up the acorns. Later in the day, the women stopped to shell some of the acorns before leaving the oak groves; this made a lighter and less bulky load of acorns to carry home, where they could be stored for a year or more. Those that were not shelled, often hundreds of pounds, were also brought home and stored for future use.

Acorns cannot be eaten without careful preparation. Before the nuts could be cooked, the women dried them and ground them into flour using big stone bowls called mortars, with stone grinders called pestles. Acorns contain tannic acid, which tastes bitter and is toxic (poisonous) to humans. The Cahuillas had learned how to remove the acid by a process called leaching. To leach the flour, the women dug a shallow pit in the earth, lined it with grass, and spread the acorn meal on top of the grass. Then they heated water and poured it over the acorn flour. They had to repeat this process several times to wash out the acid and the bitter taste it left.

After the acorn flour was leached, it could be cooked into a porridge with the consistency of thin oatmeal. Flour and water were mixed together in a watertight basket and then boiled by putting red-hot rocks in the basket. The rocks had to be stirred a bit to keep them from burning the basket. Acorn flour could also be mixed with a smaller amount of water, shaped into a kind of pancake, and roasted in hot coals. Cahuillas also obtained much of their food from mesquite plants, which grew abundantly in the desert. Two varieties of mesquite, honey mesquite and screwbean, produced edible blossoms in June and dry seedpods in July and August. Again, weather conditions affected the time when these foods ripened, so the plants had to be watched carefully. When the time came, everyone who could worked to collect the blossoms or pods. The women roasted the yellow flowers or used them to make a refreshing tea. The sweet, pulpy pods were eaten fresh. The pods, when dry, were also harvested; they were ground up and then used in porridge or shaped into cakes. The dried beans could be stored a long time, so people could eat them throughout the year at times when other foods were not available.

Cahuillas ate and used for other purposes many other plant foods—perhaps 300 different kinds in all. The women roasted tiny piñon nuts by putting small, hot coals in a shallow basket or pottery tray along with the nuts. Then they shook the tray back and forth so the coals toasted the nuts but did not burn them. Cahuillas also ate many parts of the abundant cacti found in the desert zones. The women cut cactus leaves into small pieces and boiled them to make a flavorful vegetable dish that was often mixed with other plants and herbs or meat. People also ate the fresh, juicy cactus fruits, and they ground up

cactus seeds to make a powder that was used to flavor soup or porridge.

Agave, a strikingly beautiful desert plant, provided 15-pound stalks. The edible heart, stalks, and leaves were baked for a day or two; this long cooking process dried out the sweet, delicious agave so that it could be stored for a long time. Dried agave could be relied on when there were shortages of other foods. The Cahuilla also ate the roots and tubers of several plants. Potatoes are tubers commonly eaten in America today, but Cahuillas ate different tubers and roots, such as the roots of the mariposa lily and cattail. The Cahuilla diet also included many tiny, nutritious seeds from grasses and other plants. Some of these seeds softened and expanded when cooked with water to make a porridge.

Most of the plant foods were gathered by the women, although the men helped at the busiest harvest times, when the acorns and mesquite were ready to be picked. Women would often spend an entire day on a walking and collecting trip, usually accompanied by some of their children, who helped with the work. Together, they would pick up many vegetables and fruits, or perhaps a quart of tiny seeds. To collect seeds, they used a racquet-shaped seed beater, made like an open basket with a handle. Each woman hit her seed beater against the stalks and leaves of plants to dislodge the seeds, catching them as they fell in a basketry tray. Then she would toss the seeds into a much larger carrying basket worn on her back and continue beating the plants for seeds.

Women (especially the older ones who were not strong enough to go out on day-long collecting trips) and children were responsible for the cooking. Nuts and seeds required the most preparation. Some of them had to be parched (roasted) in the shallow trays, and then they had to be ground up. A woman's grinding ability was seen as a measure of her character. After grinding, the flour was sifted to get rid of any lumps and then cooked into a porridge. Porridges, soups, and stews were boiled in baskets with hot rocks taken directly out of a fire or in clay pots put on top of a fire. The women roasted some foods directly over a fire and also baked foods in pits lined with coals or rocks taken red-hot from a fire.

*The beavertail cactus, which grew abundantly in the low desert environmental zone, was an important source of food for the Cahuillas. Its leaves, fruits, and seeds could be eaten.*

*Seeds were a nutritious and important food for the Cahuillas. A woman gathered seeds by beating grasses and bushes with a racquet-shaped beater. She held a traylike basket to catch the seeds as they fell. Then she tossed the seeds into a larger basket slung in a carrying net on her back. The net is suspended from the woman's forehead.* Top right: *A seed beater.* Bottom right: *A carrying net.*

To start a fire, Cahuillas used a fire drill. Each drill consisted of a stick that was held vertically and twirled fast on top of a small, flat piece of wood that acted as a hearth. The rapid drilling produced friction and heat, which ignited tiny sticks placed under the drill to act as tinder. Once the tinder caught fire, it could be used to start a larger fire.

Each woman owned her own set of food preparation and cooking equipment, such as parching trays, mortars, pestles, sifting and storage baskets, pots, baskets, serving dishes, and la-dles. She made most of her pots and baskets herself, but her husband made heavy stone and wooden implements for her. Women who were especially skilled at basket making or pottery making were recognized as fine artists. Older craftswomen could occasionally specialize in making baskets or pots, instead of spending time on food preparation, if there were other family members to attend to these chores.

The busiest time of year was from April to early November, when most plants ripened and had to be picked and

*(continued on page 34)*

# RELATIVES

The Cahuilla valued relatives highly. "I am related everywhere," they would say proudly, if they had gained relatives from far and wide through good marriages. One of their two major marriage rules was that two people could not marry if they were related in any way through people in the past five generations. Most Americans do not know who their great-great-great-grandmother was, but all Cahuillas would have known who theirs was.

Relatives were so important that the Cahuilla kept track of them very carefully. Their language had many terms to help them differentiate various relatives. The English language has only a few terms for male relatives: uncle, grandfather, father, brother, and son. It has a few terms for female relatives: aunt, grandmother, mother, sister, and daughter. The English word "cousin" is used for both male and female relatives who are children of an aunt and uncle.

The Cahuilla had 65 terms for various relatives. Some of these distinguished between relatives whom we call by the same name. For the Cahuilla it was important to know whether some relatives were older or younger or whether they were related through the family of one's father or one's mother. For example, the English word "brother" applies to brothers who are younger or older than yourself, but Cahuillas called their younger brothers *yuuly* and their older brothers *pas*. In English your father's father and mother's father are both called "grandfather." But if you were a Cahuilla you would call your father's father *qa?* and your mother's father *qwa?*.

This chart shows the Cahuilla terms that would be used for the members of a person's family.

*Three generations of Cahuilla women, photographed by W. D. Strong in 1924.*

| Cahuilla | Relationship | English |
| --- | --- | --- |
| qa? | father's father | grandfather |
| | father's mother | grandmother |
| | father's father's brother | great-uncle |
| | father's mother's sister | great-aunt |
| qwa? | mother's father | grandfather |
| su? | mother's mother | grandmother |
| kex | father's mother's brother | great-uncle |
| | father's father's sister | great-aunt |
| pas | older brother | brother |
| | mother's older sister's son | cousin |
| yuuly | younger brother | brother |
| | mother's younger sister's son | cousin |
| | father's younger sister's son | cousin |
| nes | older sister | sister |
| | mother's older sister | aunt |
| | mother's older sister's daughter | cousin |
| | father's older brother's daughter | cousin |
| | father's older brother's wife | aunt |
| ne?is | younger sister | sister |
| | mother's younger sister's daughter | cousin |
| | father's younger brother's daughter | cousin |
| mas | father's younger brother | uncle |
| kum | father's older brother | uncle |
| pa | father's sister | aunt |
| | mother's brother's wife | aunt |
| yis | mother's younger sister | aunt |
| | father's sister's husband | uncle |
| tas | mother's brother | uncle |
| | father's sister's husband | uncle |
| nyuku | father's sister's child | cousin |
| | mother's brother's child | cousin |

(continued from page 31)

prepared for storage immediately. A variety of game animals were hunted at that time as well. Many fruits, seeds, and flowers were dried in the sun so they could be saved for winter, when fresh foods were not available. Common sights in every Cahuilla community were huge, three- to five-foot wide granary baskets holding dried plant foods. These granaries were made of arrowweed or willow twigs and sealed with mud. After a big harvest, each granary would be full, containing several bushels of acorns, mesquite, or other dried plant foods. The food was tempting to squirrels and other rodents, so the granaries were sealed and placed out of reach on tall platforms, on rooftops, or on large boulders. Some foods, especially grass seeds, were also stored in sealed pots.

In addition to the many plant foods they ate, the Cahuillas ate the meat of many animals, birds, and insects to add flavor, protein, and fat to their diets. Animal skins were also needed for clothing, carrying bags, blankets, and other items used daily.

Three large game animals—mule deer, mountain sheep, and antelope (pronghorn deer) were considered the most valuable game because they tasted so good and provided so much meat. They could be hunted all year, although they lived in different environmental zones at different times of the year. For example, in the cold of winter, the deer moved to the canyons of the high desert to be warm. Cahuillas could hunt them readily there because many of their communities were located in canyons, too. Hunting all three of the big animals required endurance and skill; men did almost all the hunting, and they were trained in hunting skills from an early age. Men who were good enough hunters to provide food not only for their own families but also for ceremonial occasions when the whole community would feast were particularly well liked.

Cahuilla men generally used bows and arrows to shoot animals. They made their own arrow shafts from the stems and branches of cane, sagebrush, and arrowweed. They fastened stone and wooden points to the tips of the shafts and attached three feathers with animal sinew to the other ends of the shafts for stability in flight.

The knowledge of how to use and make arrows was a gift to the Cahuilla people from their creator, Mukat. This legend, told by Francisco Patencio, explains how the Cahuilla learned to make arrows.

After the moon maiden had gone away, Mukat began teaching the people. He taught them to shoot rocks from split sticks toward each other by snapping the stones from the sticks. Then he made the cane grow. This is what he made the arrow sticks from. It was cut while somewhat green, then dried. Some dried crooked, and then the people took a certain dark stone and cut grooves in it. It was used for straightening the arrow sticks. The stone was heated red-hot. The people wet the arrow with saliva in their mouths. Then by twisting and turning and pulling the arrow through the stone's slots, it became perfectly straight.

When the arrow was finished, Mukat made the arrowhead, or point. It was made in his lungs, and came out of his mouth. When he was making the arrowheads they were heard rattling in his lungs.

The legend also describes how the people began to shoot each other with the arrows, a recognition that death was a reality for humans. But in actuality, Cahuillas used arrows for hunting far more than for battles. They also used other methods of killing game. Sometimes hunters crept up close enough to club game animals instead of using bows and arrows. They also used traps and nets to catch small game.

*Large granary baskets used for storing dried plant foods were made by men from willow twigs. The baskets were placed on platforms to protect their contents from rodents and other animals.*

*A Cahuilla man chipping stone to make an arrowhead.*

Men had to know the habits of each type of animal in order to kill it. They used different hunting techniques for each animal, depending on these habits. Deer were most often hunted by a single man. Dressed in a deerskin with an antlered headpiece, he crept up close enough to kill the deer. He often used arrows tipped with poison made from the venom of black widow spiders or rattlesnakes, or even spoiled meat. The poison did not kill the deer, but it made the animal sick. Then it was easy for the hunter to walk up to it and finish off the job.

Mountain sheep were the most dangerous animals to hunt because they usually lived on tall, steep cliffs. Hunters had to watch their footing in this dangerous territory. They usually hid in well-camouflaged blinds at a water hole and shot arrows at the mountain sheep when they came to drink.

Hunting antelope required a different method because antelope could run very fast, up to 70 miles an hour. The Cahuilla men favored hunting them with a relay chase; when a herd was spotted in a canyon, several dozen men stood in a long line along the canyon floor. They took turns chasing the pronghorns to frighten them into running along a path. The path sent them into a part of the canyon that was a dead end. Sometimes the antelope got so tired they just stopped running. When the animals could go no farther and were standing still, whether because their path was blocked or because they were exhausted, the hunters could easily shoot them with arrows or club them.

Small animals, such as rabbits, rats, mice, squirrels, and chipmunks, were abundant. Cahuillas actually ate more meat from these small animals than from the big ones because these animals were so plentiful and easy to catch. In winter, when few plants were ripe, rabbit meat was especially important. Sometimes Cahuilla men hunted them with bow and arrow, but they also used curved wooden throwing sticks that looked like boomerangs but did not come back to the thrower. Instead, the hunter threw the stick low to the ground to break the rabbit's legs and then he retrieved both the rabbit and the stick. A skilled hunter could hit rabbits from 50 yards away.

Cahuillas had other methods for catching small game. Sometimes they caught the animals in snares or traps. Old men often hunted small animals this way because it was not as dangerous or tiring as the big-game hunting done by younger men. They sometimes used pit traps, which were deep holes covered with brush into which animals fell. When many rabbits and other small animals were needed for a ceremonial feast, all the men, women, and children cooperated to catch hundreds at a time. They spread huge nets of rope made from plant fiber in an arc shape and then chased small animals into the net. The rabbits, squirrels, rats, and other animals could be clubbed after they were caught this way. Then the men butchered the animals, and the women boiled, roasted, or baked the meat. The rabbit skins were cut into strips and woven into soft, warm blankets or robes.

Birds were also an important food, and quail especially were considered a delicacy. They were easily captured with nets, traps, snares, throwing sticks, or bow and arrow. Women often covered the entire carcass of a quail in wet clay, then baked it, and finally cracked the clay shell open to produce steaming hot, tasty morsels of meat. Snakes, particularly rattlesnakes, and insects such as ants, grasshoppers, cicadas, and larval moths were all eaten, too. Cahuillas also ate fish, although in recent years, after Lake Cahuilla became dry, not many were available.

An important part of Cahuilla life was being a social person. Every person belonged to one of two groups: the Wildcats, who were believed to be the descendants of the beings made by Mukat; or the Coyotes, who were believed to descend from Temayawut's beings. A person whose father was a Wildcat would also be a Wildcat, and a person whose father was a Coyote would be a Coyote. Everyone who was a member of the Wildcat group had to marry someone from the Coyote group, and

*A skilled hunter could hit a rabbit or other small animal with a throwing stick from a distance of 50 yards. This stick is 25½ inches long.*

everyone from the Coyote group had to marry a Wildcat. There were also ceremonies in which Wildcats had to perform one part of the ritual while Coyotes had to perform another part in order for the ritual to be complete.

The Wildcat and Coyote groups were further divided into several smaller groups or clans. Membership in a clan also depended on the clan membership of a person's father. Girls and boys both belonged to the clan of their father. A man's property rights and sometimes his personal belongings and ownership of the rights to perform certain rituals were passed down to his sons. Each clan had its own name, for example, Wanikik (literally, swirling water) or Kauisik (people of the rocks). Each clan recognized a male ancestor of everyone in the clan. The clan was a tightly knit group, even though it might be so large that some people in it would not know exactly how they were related to some others. For the Cahuilla, clan membership was the equivalent of our concept of nationality, because it provided a person's primary identity—like being an American or a Canadian.

Each clan owned its own territory with many natural resources, and only clan members could use those resources unless they gave someone else permission. Altogether, a clan might own an area as big as 600 square miles (half the size of Rhode Island). A clan established the boundaries of its own land, sometimes by using petroglyphs (pictures incised or scratched into rocks, or pecked into rocks by hammering with stones), stones, or specific geographic features. Usually the clan area formed an uneven wedge shape that included land in all four environmental zones, from the low and high desert through the transition zone and into the high mountains. This made it possible for the clan to use all the zones to obtain food. Sometimes all the men in the clan would unite to protect these resources against intruders from other clans.

The clan's unity made it a force in food getting and problem solving. The men in the clan could join together to hunt. All the political and religious leaders in a clan could confer when an emergency occurred; they could combine their knowledge, strength, and supernatural power to deal with disaster. Finally, most of the people in a clan sometimes came together in one place for religious ceremonies.

Each clan was made up of smaller groups, or lineages. Usually there were from 3 to 10 lineages in each clan. Every person belonged to the same lineage as his or her father. As in clans, each lineage had a father figure who was the ancestor of all lineage members. But in lineages, this was a man who had lived not too long ago, who was known to and remembered by lineage members, a man who had had many children and grandchildren. The male ancestor was the father, grandfather, great-grandfather, uncle, or brother of everyone in the lineage. All lineage members knew their relationship to one another. Lin-

*A petroglyph, or rock picture. The design was pecked, or carved, by hammering with a sharp stone. Petroglyphs were often used to mark the boundaries of a clan's territory.*

eages owned their own land, food resources, and sacred places within the clan territory. They also controlled special stories and songs that only lineage members had the right to tell or sing. Additionally, lineages could own the right to have their own members hold certain ceremonial and political positions; the lineages of a single clan would divide these roles so that each lineage owned at least one.

Lineages were important groups in Cahuilla society because each had its own community. All males and all female children in a community belonged to the same lineage. Because Wildcats could not marry Wildcats or Coyotes marry other Coyotes, the women in a Cahuilla community were always mem-

bers of lineages from the opposite group. When a woman was married, she went to live with her husband in the community of his lineage. Thus, a typical Cahuilla community consisted of elderly men who were brothers, their wives, and their sons and nephews, together with their wives and children. Because lineage members lived together, they and their spouses frequently ate, cooked, hunted, collected plants, held ceremonies, and played games together. A person's friends were all a part of the lineage community, too.

The location of a community depended upon the environment. People needed to live near water, food, and raw materials, and they wanted to live

*The Indians dug deep wells to tap underground water sources.*

in a moderate climate. Most settlements were in the high or low desert areas. Canyons in the high desert were frequently used because they were likely to have sources of fresh water, which also meant abundant food resources nearby, and because the canyon walls protected people from the harshest weather. Every community had at least one nearby spring; Cahuillas also dug deep wells using wooden shovels in order to ensure a good water supply for their homes.

When the people of a lineage chose a new location to build their houses, the settlement land and the surrounding area belonged to that lineage. No other group could use the area without permission. The lineage members would share the surrounding territory with other lineages in their clan, but the nearest lineage settlement was usually several miles from their own. Clan and lineage ownership of land and wild resources enabled Cahuillas to schedule who would collect which foods at what time and thus control the food supply. They made sure that they did not exhaust a particular food source so that there would be enough roots, seeds, and young animals to provide food the following year.

Communities were inhabited all year, although during the harvest season some people would leave temporarily to camp near a particular food resource. Half the people in a community might move to the acorn or piñon groves at harvest time; in August, many men would go away to harvest and process agave, returning with hundreds of pounds of food that could be stored for later use. Men sometimes moved high into the mountains to hunt for extended periods.

Each community had a sweathouse and one community would have a ceremonial house that served the entire clan. The ceremonial house was the largest building in the community. It was usually built next to a permanent water source. The ceremonial house was the site of all religious rituals and events. Political meetings, curing rituals, and recreational activities often took place there or nearby as well. It was usually dome shaped and was often as large as 50 feet in diameter.

The interior of the ceremonial house was divided into two sections. The smaller section was the sacred sanctuary where the *maiswat* (ceremonial bundle) was kept. Inside the larger section of the ceremonial house was a ceremonial dance floor and space for the congregation to sit. Outside, in front of the ceremonial house, was a second, fenced dance floor and benches on which the participants could sit. There was also a cooking area attached to the house, where food was prepared for the people participating in ceremonies and for their guests. The *net*, the community's political and religious leader, lived in or near the ceremonial house. That way he could supervise the activities that occurred there and care for the maiswat.

The sweathouse was a meeting place for the men in the community. It served as a sauna for ritual sweating, health, and as a club for social and religious purposes. While the men sat inside, their talk often turned to important community matters, so the sweathouse was also a site for political decision making. A typical matter that might come up for discussion in the sweathouse was the scheduling of food-collecting activities for a season.

Every family had its own house. Cahuilla men were responsible for building the houses, and they knew several different ways to construct them. Sometimes they used caves and added shelters made of brush at the front to provide more room. Caves remained cool in the intense heat of the summer and were easy to heat with fire in winter because the dense walls kept out the wind. Sometimes the men built cone-shaped houses of cedar bark. Most houses were circular, with domed roofs, although a few were rectangular.

*Every Cahuilla community had a sweathouse, where men gathered for social and ritual steam baths. Here they discussed important matters and also held healing and purification ceremonies.*

In size they ranged from very small shelters just big enough for a few people to lie down in—about the size of a 4-person tent—to fairly large structures, about 150 to 300 feet square, the size of a living room today. Men built houses from a variety of materials. Usually, they set wooden posts forked at the top in the ground to support the roof; then they thatched the walls and roof with palm fronds, arrowweed, tule reeds, or some other flexible plant stems. Sometimes they plastered the walls with adobe (sun-baked mud) or shored them up with hard-packed desert sand. They left one or more holes in the roof to allow smoke from indoor fires to escape.

Often two or three closely related families would build their houses in a cluster and connect them with covered walkways and walls that served as windbreaks. These provided protection from the hot sun or biting winds while

*Maria Los Angeles outside her traditional home, a rectangular structure, on Cahuilla Reservation.*

the people worked outside their homes. Many daily tasks, such as basket weaving and cooking, were performed out-of-doors.

The first anthropologist to write about the Cahuilla, David Prescott Barrows, described the interior of a Cahuilla house in 1900:

> At one side of the door within lies the woman's broad metate [grinding stone] and her mortar for crushing seeds, both kept covered with a mat or cloth. At the other side of the door stands the brown *tinaja* or water jar . . . brought full each morning from the spring. In the center of the floor is the hearth with its few blackened cooking pots; perhaps a beautifully woven baby hammock swings from the ceiling. . . . The usual bed is simply an untanned rawhide and a blanket spread on the floor. Supplies of food are kept in earthen *ollas* [clay storage jars] or beautiful grass baskets, and pieces of jerked [dried] meat and bundles of herbs, together with innumerable household articles, are tucked into the sides of the thatching. There is little to become disarranged.

Inside a house lived a family, the smallest group to which a Cahuilla could belong and the primary social unit of Cahuilla society. The family members living together might include grandparents, their children, and their grandchildren.

An important concern of a family was to arrange a good marriage for its young men and women. The young people themselves had little influence on their parents' choice. A marriage created a social and economic bond between the bride and groom's families. Therefore, the young people's parents would carefully consider the choice of a future spouse in order to find the most advantageous family to gain as relatives. In the Cahuilla social system, a person's relatives were the people with whom he or she most often talked, ate, held ceremonies, or went hunting and food collecting. Therefore, it was necessary to make sure that any relatives gained through marriage were desirable people not only in terms of their personal qualities but also in their ability to create social and economic ties to other lineages and clans in other areas. Particularly desirable were those who could help obtain foods that were ordinarily hard to get.

Cahuillas had two important rules that governed who could marry whom. First, Wildcats had to marry Coyotes, and Coyotes had to marry Wildcats. Second, a person could not marry someone related to him or her within five generations.

In addition to considerations about the families being joined through marriage, the personal qualities of the young people were important. A young girl's parents sought for her a future husband who was a good hunter and food provider, a young man who was respectful of his elders and mindful of his responsibilities to his relatives. A young man who showed leadership

*Dolores Patencio, a Cahuilla woman, making a basket in the 1930s. She is using traditional plant materials, which she gathered and prepared herself, and traditional techniques and designs.*

abilities in rituals or medicine was also considered a good catch, especially if he was in line to inherit a political or ceremonial role. A young boy's parents chose for him a future wife who was hardworking and an efficient cook, a young woman who would be respectful of her elders and fulfill her responsibilities to her relatives. She had to be able to get along with her future husband's family because she would live with them after the marriage.

In arranging a marriage, the parents also took into account the reputation of the other family. They might not want their children to marry someone beneath them in rank. And a marriage was unlikely between members of two families that had quarreled in the past.

From the time parents arranged a marriage, the families would give each other gifts of food and other items. This gift exchange was such a valued activity that the families would constantly remind the young couple of their responsibilities in helping to carry out the exchanges. The young husband had to hunt game animals for his wife's family until he and his wife had their first child. This was part of the large gift traditionally given by the man's family to the new bride's family. Also, all the young man's relatives constantly gave gifts to the relatives of the young woman and received gifts in return. Whenever the boy's relatives visited the community of the girl's family, they would be fed, entertained, and given gifts; in return, they brought gifts of food and household items with them. When they returned home they shared the food gifts they had received with all their other relatives. The flow of economic goods between intermarried families was frequent and long lasting.

The bride always left her family and community to go live in her new husband's community, often 20 to 50 miles away. There she would have to make new friends. This could be a lonely time for her, because at first she would know few people because most of the village would not be related to her. After a while, though, she would start to fit in. The children born to her and her husband would belong to the same side of Cahuilla society as her husband (either Wildcat or Coyote). When these children grew up, the sons would bring home brides, but the daughters would marry and move away.

Divorce was possible but it did not occur very often. Because the families had so much at stake in the union of the young couple, they tried to convince the bride and groom to stay together in spite of difficulties. Even if the bride ran away from her husband her family would return her and urge her not to divorce her husband. However, if the husband was very abusive or if the young woman failed to have children or was horribly lazy, a divorce could be granted. Then the bride's family would have to return the gifts they had received prior to the marriage, or an equivalent amount, and the bride would return to her parents.

The bond between two families joined by marriage was so strong that even death might not break it. If a husband died, his unmarried brother or other male relative could marry his widow. If the wife died, her unmarried sister or female cousin might marry the widower. (A man could not have two wives.) This remarriage would keep the interfamily bond going and ensure that children had two parents to care for them.

All groups in Cahuilla society were based on these relationships. Every person was a Wildcat or a Coyote, a member of a clan, a lineage, and a family. The lineages of each clan interacted with each other often, especially during the winter. At that time, in the pause between the busiest food-getting seasons, the Cahuilla gathered to perform many religious ceremonies—ceremonies that would emphasize the bonds of relationship among them and ensure the food supply for the coming year. ▲

Marcos—Palm Canyon Cahuilla, *photographed by Edward S. Curtis in 1924. Marcos Belardo was the paxaa? at Agua Caliente Reservation when this picture was taken.*

# MANAGING THE SOCIAL AND PHYSICAL WORLDS

In the Cahuilla social and physical worlds, the creative force ?iva?a made the actions of people, animals, and nature unpredictable because it was uncertain itself. Cahuillas explained unusual events by pointing to the power of ?iva?a. To cope with the uncertainty of ?iva?a and to ensure social stability, they had clear values and followed a set of rules about how to behave. Their values and rules, which were stated in the sacred songs performed at rituals, were based on the way the world was in the time of Mukat and the nukatem (the early beings). As Francisco Patencio said, "When I speak of the songs of the people being against them, it means that the songs were the laws of the people. These songs were remembered. They could not forget, because they were always singing at the ceremonial houses. . . . When anyone did something that was not in the law,

the Indian people would say that 'the song is against them.' Their own people [family] would not recognize them if the songs were against them. That was our law." The past was an important model for Cahuilla behavior. Mukat had created the "proper" social system. Cahuillas knew that this system was the one that worked the best and that they should strive to use it. They listened to the songs and stories that told of the early days in order to decide how to act and to interpret what they experienced from day to day. On the basis of these songs, people decided important matters, such as when to engage in rituals, when to produce rock paintings, baskets, images of the dead, and exchange goods, how to deal with hostile groups or new and strange events, and whether to go to battle. Although they honored tradition, Cahuillas also valued innovations that came about through discoveries of how power could be used or how tradition could be interpreted.

Cahuillas were always expected to show deference to and respect for their elders because older people had greater knowledge of history and were in the best position to know what was right according to tradition. This knowledge was important in the case of natural disasters that occurred only occasionally or when people needed to resolve conflicts with others. As children learned skills and values from their grandparents, they learned, too, that older people knew much more than young people.

Another personal characteristic valued by the Cahuilla was industriousness. People who were diligent and hardworking were particularly desirable as prospective spouses. Industrious people could cope with both the physical and social worlds because they worked hard to save enough food for times of shortage and helped care for those in need. Cahuillas considered it a disgrace for people to be lazy and admired people who worked steadily, carefully, and productively. Industrious people demonstrated the same qualities that Mukat had used to create the world and humans, so he was their model for behavior.

Another valued behavior was reciprocity, giving in return as much as or more than one has received. Repayment could be prompt, or it could come long after the original gift. Prompt re-

ciprocity occurred when a marriage was arranged and the groom's family visited and exchanged gifts with the bride's family. Guests at all Cahuilla rituals were required to bring gifts, and the hosts would give them food, baskets, nets, shell ornaments, and other presents in return. Ritual itself was believed to be the humans' gift to the nukatem to reciprocate for the spirits' help in getting food and other necessities. Reciprocity was such an important principle that Cahuilla people would not even think of thanking someone for a gift. They believed it was natural to receive gifts and to give more gifts in return. Cahuillas looked down on or laughed at anyone who was stingy or who received a gift without giving one in return. The rule of reciprocity helped people get along together, and their mutual gift giving helped them manage the physical world. A family or lineage that experienced a food shortage could rely on receiving food from people who knew that their gifts would be repaid some year when they needed food.

Cahuillas also valued order, precision, and dependability. They based these values on the orderly, precise way in which Mukat had created people, as opposed to the careless way in which Temayawut had made his beings. People realized that the lesson of this story was to do things carefully and well. They realized that their actions had consequences for all other parts of the world system, so the well-being of

(continued on page 57)

# COILED BASKETS AND POTS

The art of basketry was a gift to the Cahuilla from Menily the moon maiden. Men made heavy, openwork baskets used for gathering plant foods and large baskets for storing food. Women made fine coiled baskets for ceremonies and gifts, as well as those used for cooking, storing, and serving foods. Older women also made utilitarian pottery from clay they prepared themselves.

The foundation for a coiled basket was usually a bundle of deer grass, around which juncus (a marsh grass or rush) or sumac (a low tree or shrub) stems were wrapped. The women often wove designs of rattlesnakes, eagles, stars, and other sacred symbols into their baskets. They used plant materials of different colors, which they either found naturally or dyed with some natural substance. For black, for example, they buried the plant materials in sulphur- or iron-rich mud.

Basketry drew on Cahuilla women's creativity, and the ability to make fine baskets earned them wealth as well as prestige.

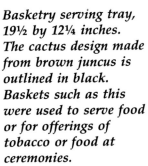

*Basketry serving tray, 19½ by 12¼ inches. The cactus design made from brown juncus is outlined in black. Baskets such as this were used to serve food or for offerings of tobacco or food at ceremonies.*

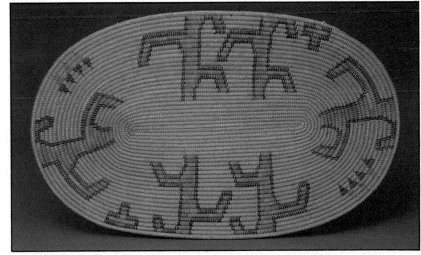

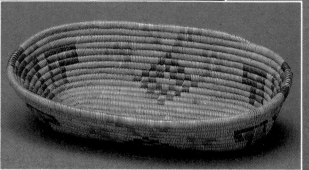

*Oval basket, 9½ inches long by 5 inches wide by 2½ inches high.*

*Tray for acorn meal, 10¾ inches in diameter and 1¾ inches high, made of white aromatic sumac coiled over a grass stem foundation. The black strands are sumac stems dyed with elderberry.*

**Above:** *Twined openwork basket, probably used for sifting acorn meal, 14 inches in diameter and 5 inches high. Men made the plain twined baskets that were used for utilitarian purposes.*

*Coiled basket, 11¼ inches diameter by 3 inches high. Cahuilla women were innovative, creative artists, and no two baskets are the same.*

Older women were usually the potters, building the vessels by coiling ropes of clay around and around a flat clay base, in much the same way as they built their baskets. They smoothed the walls first with their fingers, then shaped and thinned the walls by hitting the outside with a flat wooden paddle against a polished stone anvil held on the inside. Baking or firing hardened the clay and made the pots watertight.

**Right:** *Undecorated olla, or water jar, 10 inches high. The small mouth of an olla helped to prevent evaporation, and the narrow neck was easy to hold for carrying and pouring. Ollas were smoothed and shaped by hand only from the outside.*

**Left:** *Red-decorated olla found in a cave in Morongo Valley, 7¾ inches high, 7 inches in diameter, with a mouth 2 inches in diameter. The red designs were painted on with ground hematite, an iron-rich stone. Women often incised or painted designs on pots before firing them.*

*Right: Pottery bowl, 10 inches high, 12 inches in diameter. The mouth is 8 inches in diameter.*

*Below: Prehistoric olla, found in a cave in San Andres Canyon in about 1918, 13¾ inches high by 12½ inches in diameter.*

53

*Basket-bowl, 16¼ inches in diameter and 3¾ inches high. The design may represent cactus.*

*Camels, a faded butterfly, and other figures decorate a bowl-shaped basket, 14¼ inches in diameter by 4¼ inches high. In the 1890s the government tried to introduce camels to the California desert. The experiment failed, but not before inspiring the maker of this basket.*

Right: The snake is the
most prominent of the
designs on this basket.
Most of the other
designs are too dim to
identify, but a faded
turtle appears at top
left.

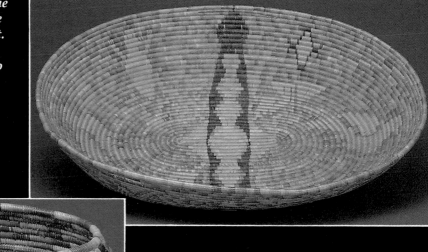

Left: A diamond-backed snake coils
around the upper half of this small
basket, only 6¼ inches in diameter and
3½ inches high, made in the early 20th
century. The diamond design on the lower
half is a visual pun calling attention to
the snake's back.

The diamond-backed
rattlesnake, a popular
design in Cahuilla
baskets, coils around
the inside and outside
of this large basket-
bowl, 16½ inches in
diameter and 7 inches
high. The tan back-
ground is willow. The
basket was made
before 1910

*Alphabet basket, 9 inches in diameter and 6¼ inches high. The basket-maker was apparently intrigued with the design possibilities of the letter shapes.*

*Miniature coiled baskets demonstrated their maker's dexterity. The basket at left is 1½ inches in diameter and 1 inch high; at right, 1¼ inches in diameter and ¾ inch high.*

*Indians winnowing wheat, tossing grains from basket to basket so the wind can carry off the chaff (husks). Industriousness was an important and highly valued trait among the Cahuilla, who believed that hard-working people were following the example of Mukat, the Creator.*

(continued from page 48)

Cahuilla society and the physical world depended upon them. Because ?iva?a was so unpredictable, people were concerned about the possible consequences from any action made in error. Therefore, they held many rituals to try to help them achieve order and precision.

In this way, people tried to manage the social and physical worlds by managing their own behavior.

Cahuillas also desired to show personal control and moderation in their behavior. They did not want to overdo anything. When they worked hard and

*An elderly Cahuilla couple, photographed in 1911. Elders were highly respected and often consulted by family and community members.*

carefully, they did not receive any extravagant rewards or recognition. They felt emotions as deeply as any people do, but they would not be flamboyant about it. They showed their feelings quietly, with dignity and reserve. Their ability to control the show of emotion was a practical help in their daily life. For example, when a hungry hunter spotted a deer after days of searching, he did not yell with joy or do anything else that would startle the deer. He was accustomed to containing himself so that he would continue calmly to stalk

the deer and succeed in bringing it home to eat.

Cahuillas valued secrecy and caution. For instance, they sometimes gave secret names to children during the naming ceremonies. They also kept secrets about other things. Many of their children's stories tell of people who could not keep a secret and therefore ended up in big trouble, so children learned from their earliest years to be careful about telling secrets. Sometimes people would keep secret the location of a hidden cache of food. If they kept the secret, then in time of shortage they could use that food; if they told other people, the food might be gone when they needed it most. Secrets thus helped protect people from witchcraft (in the case of secret names) and hunger (in the case of secret food resources).

Cahuillas who behaved correctly according to all these principles would avoid serious disputes with other members of the community. But some Cahuillas misbehaved. Some were stingy; some committed murder. If they merely made small mistakes, the gossip about them was usually enough to make them change their ways. In order to discipline a member who had misbehaved, a lineage would sing a song about that person's misbehavior at a ceremony or social gathering. This shamed the person and his or her family, embarrassing the wrongdoer into acting correctly. But when someone did something horrible enough to cause an argument between families, other members of the community would insist that someone wise and with authority make a decision about the outcome of the dispute.

In keeping with the Cahuilla's admiration of tradition and age, the people consulted for decisions were often the oldest men and women in the community. Although women, by tradition, did not play a formal role in governing the community, they were important judges of Cahuilla life. Therefore, it was the older men and some older women who spent much of their time acting together as authorities for the community. They gathered together to solve arguments between families and make decisions about the community.

People who held ceremonial and leadership roles were believed to have the authority to manage the physical and social worlds. All these religious and political leaders were men. A young man could inherit these political or religious roles from his father or from an uncle (his father's brother). These occupations, such as ceremonial doctor and ritual dancer or singer, were very difficult and time consuming. A man might specialize in being a ceremonial singer, for example, and spend most of his time memorizing and practicing long song cycles. His training would be as arduous and lengthy as an opera singer's in modern society.

These important leaders guided each lineage in ceremonial, economic, and political matters. People usually obeyed these leaders because their power had been given to them in the early times, by Mukat and the nukatem. To justify the power of these community leaders, Cahuillas cited references to them in the stories of the early times. Each lineage or clan had a net, who acted as a ceremonial leader and a judge who settled disputes. The net, always a man and usually the son of the previous net, was the key individual in Cahuilla society. He was the ceremonial leader, responsible for seeing that all rituals were performed correctly and for taking care of the ceremonial bundle and the ceremonial house. He also looked after the economic affairs of his community, determining where and when people would go to gather foods or hunt game. For example, it was the net who directed the first harvest ceremonies each year for the acorn and mesquite crops. The net was also a judge in land disputes and had to remember the lineage and clan land boundaries. He solved other disputes, too, sometimes with the help of the *paxaa?* (his assistant) and the *puvalam* (the association of shamans—men with magic powers). The net's authority was made clear in the story of the first net who managed the first ceremonial activities after the death of Mukat; this story was retold at each mourning and memorial ceremony.

The paxaa? was the net's assistant in all matters, and he played an important role in birth, initiation, death, and other rituals. By making sure that certain ritual acts were properly performed

*Francisco Patencio, a religious leader and storyteller, brother of Alejo Patencio.*

and punishing those who misbehaved during ceremonies, the paxaa? saw to it that a ceremony would be effective. He also participated fully in economic tasks, often organizing and leading hunting parties. The paxaa? was feared and respected by the people of his community. His power was justified by stories of how Coyote had acted as the first paxaa? at Mukat's memorial ceremonies.

The stories also describe how Coyote gathered materials for the first ceremonial bundle (maiswat). The maiswat was the most sacred object. It consisted of a piece of reed matting about 5 feet wide and 20 feet long, rolled to form a container for ceremonial objects. The objects in the maiswat would include

feathers used in rituals, shell beads used in ritual exchanges, a bone whistle, a sacred staff or wand, tobacco, and other items used in ceremonies. The maiswat also contained ?vi?va, the creative supernatural power that communicated with the net.

Francisco Patencio told this story in *Stories and Legends of the Palm Springs Indians*, a book he wrote in 1943 when he was in his nineties.

One day Coyote called all the people together and talked to them about honoring Mukat's grave with special decorations and having a memorial ceremony for their father. They were all willing, but some told him that they had nothing, no food, no clothes, not anything to make a memorial with. Coyote said not to mind about that because he would look for some things. He went to the ocean. The ocean was at high tide, so he waited there and lay down and went to sleep in the daytime. When he awoke he did not know how long he had slept. He jumped into the ocean and came up with three water plants: *panga me ya va*, water-apron; *panga ha quat*, watertail; and *panga mic vat*, tule reeds.

He took all those things home, and he called all the brothers and sisters. They came, because they knew these things that Coyote brought were good herbs—herbs that were useful medicine. So they came together and talked over what they were going to do, how they were going to do it, and when they were going to do it. For this was something they had never done before.

Who was to manage it, and who would attend to the ceremonials? Coyote said that he would attend to the ceremonials, and he did it. He began a song that told of the time when Mukat had come out of the ocean; then another, telling of the center of the earth, from which Mukat and Temayawut were born. Then the head men decided to set aside a few days for the memorial.

The memorial service for Mukat lasted a week. The head men decided that the first day should be a day of prayer, and all of the people agreed. It was a day of prayer for the people, their friends, their homes—for all of the people, both living and dead.

This ceremony was managed by three head men. One had charge of everything pertaining to the religious ceremony and assigned tasks to the second and third head men. The second was in charge of distributing the food to the people. The third head man would smoke the sacred pipe, blowing the smoke to the north

three times the first day, three times to the west and south the second day, and nine times in all directions the third day. The fourth day was set apart for a day of rest, and on the fifth day they made the images of the dead. The paxaa? attended to blowing the sacred smoke. At this first ceremony, the paxaa? was Coyote. On the fifth day he called all the people to be quiet. Then he blew the sacred smoke and called out prayer, and all of the people, especially the old ones, who belonged there went into the ceremonial house.

The tule reeds that Coyote had brought grew so very tall that no one could find the end of them, so the head man of the ceremony cut a portion, and inside the reed bundle he put the feather of an eagle, some Indian money made of strung shells, a pipe and some tobacco, and a certain rock that is sometimes red, yellow, blue, or black. This was the first maiswat, the sacred bundle.

The tule was one of the good gifts that Coyote brought the people. A part of the tule that had been used for

*A ceremonial clay pipe about 6¼ inches long was uncovered in the southern California desert in 1916. This drawing was made the following year by Edward H. Davis, a rancher from southern California who became interested in objects made by Indians.*

the maiswat was used to make an image to represent the father, Mukat. On the sixth day the people burned the image and scattered seed from the first plants that grew from the ground where Mukat was buried, in memory of their father.

These head men were great men, men of much power, and if anything that should have been done was not done right or was not done well, they knew it at once. And this is all of the first ceremony in memory of Mukat. Now the descendants of these first people are living here among us yet. These men had charge of the ceremonies until recent years.

The ritual singer, called the *haunik*, was also respected by his entire community. He could be young or old, but he always possessed a great deal of talent and the ability to remember song cycles lasting as long as 12 hours. He owned the right to perform certain songs that were needed for major ceremonies and played an especially important role in initiating young people. It was the haunik who taught them the songs associated with their lineage and instructed them in proper adult behavior.

The *ngengewish* were the ritual dancers, men who possessed grace, stamina, and a sense of mimicry, rhythm, timing, and imagination. Their ceremonial role was particularly important because they brought to life the stories of the early people, the nukatem. One dance they performed was the eagle dance. William Duncan Strong witnessed an eagle dance, discussed it with the Cahuilla people, and described it in his 1929 book *Aboriginial Society in Southern California*. The eagle dance was usually performed at the end of a memorial ceremony. It was announced by a ceremonial official who twirled a bullroarer over his head. This instrument consisted of rope with a piece of wood attached to it. The distinctive whirring noise of the bullroarer signaled that the dance was about to begin. Then all the people would form a circle outside the ceremonial house. The official would step into the center of the circle, and a ngengewish would run out of the dance house and into the center of the circle. This eagle dancer wore a skirt and a headdress both made of eagle feathers, and he held two short sticks in his hands. His face and neck were covered with white clay. As he knelt in the center of the circle, he stared up at the sun for more than a minute. Then he moved slowly around the circle, imitating the actions—flight, sitting, hopping, and alighting—of an eagle and hitting his sticks together to direct the rhythm of the people in singing. Suddenly, he would begin to whirl faster and faster, accompanied by the men and women who were singing and dancing in line around the circle. As he whirled, his feather skirt was lifted up by the air so that it straightened out. Finally, the ceremonial official would shout out to signal that the last song had been sung, and then the dancer would suddenly stop whirling and run into the dance house. Sometimes other ngengewish would also dance, always one at a time.

The shamans, called puul or pa?vu?ul depending on the strength of their magical powers, were able to control the world not only with their power to diagnose and cure illness but also through other abilities. They received instructions, songs, dances, and supernatural power from spirit guardians that resided inside their bodies. Those known as pa?vu?ul were so powerful they could even transform themselves into other types of beings, such as bear, mountain lion, eagle, or other animals. Shamans had to prove constantly to the people of the community that they continued to have power. They did many amazing acts to demonstrate their power. Sometimes a shaman would reaffirm his power at the witches' dance by pulling his spirit guardian from his throat or nose. Then he might appear to eat hot coals without harming himself or pull out his hair and then return it to his body.

All the shamans belonged to an informal association. This group worked together with the net and the paxaa? to make decisions for the community, especially in time of disaster. The economic role of the shamans was also critical. When there was a scarcity of food, or even the possibility of scarcity, a shaman would draw a miniature food-producing tree such as an oak from his hand during a public performance. This

*Tepharino Apapas, a Cahuilla haunik (ritual singer) and ngengewish (ritual dancer), photographed in 1911.*

would ensure a plentiful acorn crop that season. The shaman was expected to help crops by controlling rain and other weather conditions with a rain song. The shaman was also able to use his power to discover the location of animals for the hunters, and even to en- courage the animals to make themselves available for the hunters.

The shamans also participated in every Cahuilla ritual, usually to make sure the ceremonial house was clear of witches and other evil spirits. In addition to controlling the spiritual world,

*Ambrosia, a Cahuilla shaman, prepares to perform the Fire Eating Ceremony to demonstrate his supernatural power. He will appear to put hot coals in his mouth.*

the shamans were responsible for the social world during ceremonies. All the people at a ceremony knew the shamans would take action against them if they disturbed the success of the ceremony, so they were very careful not to start an argument or create any disturbances.

Shamans were also able to predict the future by reading signs given by birds, animals, and heavenly bodies. For example, when a shaman saw a falling star, he knew that a person's soul was lost. Then he would try to find out whose soul it was so that he could return the soul to the person before a soul-catching spirit found it.

Through good behavior and with the help of community leaders such as shamans and the net, the Cahuillas coped with the uncertainties of their environment. In song, story, and ceremony, they repeated the rules and emphasized the values that helped them keep their balance in an unpredictable world. ▲

A Cahuilla Child, *photographed by Edward S. Curtis in 1924.*

# RITUALS
## OF
# LIFE

When a young Cahuilla man killed a deer for the first time, all the people in his community joined in a celebration. In the 1920s, the anthropologist William Duncan Strong was present when such a ceremony took place. We know a great deal about Cahuilla rituals because Strong observed and recorded many of their ceremonies.

The young man's parents took his deer to the ceremonial house in their community. Then all the people arrived bringing food for a feast. A puul sang a song thanking the deer for allowing itself to be killed. The puul's song told the deer to go to the *telmekic*, the place where the spirits of dead beings stay. He asked the deer to give a good report about the young hunter to Pemtem-weha, the Cahuilla god of the hooved animals, so that the young man would have good fortune on future hunting trips.

Then the deer was skinned, and a man held up the skin and shouted "he! he! he!" three times and puffed his breath to the north. The men cooked the deer meat, and the young man shared it with his family and friends. A young unmarried man was supposed to share the game he had killed. Sharing and generosity were and still are important values taught to Cahuillas at a very young age.

Similar ceremonies were held for other important foods, such as the first acorn, agave, mesquite, and piñon crops collected each year. Anybody who ate mesquite before the time appointed by the net would be punished. As soon as the mesquite ripened, the net sent someone to gather a little bit of it. The person brought the mesquite to the ceremonial house, where the whole community gathered to eat a portion of it. Everyone came with extra food with which to make a feast. They expressed their appreciation to Mukat, the creator, for providing the mesquite. This ensured that future crops would be bountiful and harvested in a way that benefited everyone. When the ceremony was over, the net declared that harvesting season was open and the people could start collecting the mesquite. A similar ceremony was held for the first appearance each season of other important plant foods.

Cahuillas celebrated the first deer (as well as the first mountain sheep and antelope) in a young man's hunting career and the first harvest of several plants because these foods were of vital importance in their lives. They observed other rituals as well—the ritual to bring rain or otherwise influence the weather, an eagle-killing ritual to honor the perpetuation of each lineage and provide feathers for sacred garments, and many rituals celebrating individuals' changes in status.

Curing rituals were among the most important ceremonies in a Cahuilla's life. The people distinguished between illnesses that were due to natural causes, such as a wound from an accident or snakebite, and those that were the result of supernatural causes such as witchcraft, punishment by powerful beings for breaking important rules, or evil spirits. Diagnosis and healing were done by shamans, who had medical knowledge as well as powers obtained from supernatural sponsors. The shaman would diagnose the disease by consulting the spirit that gave him his power. Then he proceeded to cure the disease with natural or supernatural means. He could extract the disease by sucking the patient's body and apparently removing an object such as a stone, which he would display as the cause of the illness and then dispose of. He also sang special songs and used natural aids such as massage and herbal remedies to complete such cures.

Every society has its own rituals. In the United States today, being chris-

*A Cahuilla ngengewish, or ritual dancer, performs the eagle ritual, which honors the perpetuation of a family lineage. The eagle dance often closes a memorial ceremony.*

tened, graduating from high school or college, getting married, and attending a funeral are rituals that many people go through. We know a great deal about Cahuilla rituals because they were observed or described by various people in the first half of the 20th century. Mukat's funeral was the first funeral known to the Cahuilla, and its story was passed down through the generations. This is the way Alejo Patencio told the story to W. D. Strong in 1926.

Mukat fell sick. He sang to himself, "My body became cold, swollen and weak." All his creatures stayed in the ceremonial house watching him. Coyote was his nurse and tended him, but Mukat became even more ill. Mukat called all his creatures and said, "When I die Coyote will try to eat me, for he is planning to do this while you sleep. Therefore, when I am dead tell Coyote to go after the eastern fire, which I drew from my heart to light my pipe. When he is gone gather all kinds of wood, dig a hole, and prepare to burn my body."

Then Mukat died. His creatures all cried that there was nothing with which to burn their father, and they asked Coyote to go after the eastern fire. When he was out of sight, they prepared the pit, kindled the fire, dragged the body of Mukat to the fire, and put it on the burning wood. Mukat's body burned. Coyote looked back and saw the smoke. "I thought that might be the way!" he said, and he quickly ran back. Coyote jumped over the other creatures and grabbed

*Pedro Chino, a Cahuilla pa?vu?ul, or shaman.*

Mukat's heart. He ran away and swallowed it.

Then all Mukat's creatures began to wonder how they could make an image of their father. Coyote said, "I will show you." He went into the ocean and got the things needed to make the image of Mukat. Then he began to make the image of his father. The creatures sang a song about moving the image, standing it up, carrying it to the fire, placing it on the pile of wood, lighting the fire, the smoking, the burning, the crumbling of the last ashes, and the last of the burning. Then, covering the ashes with dirt, they sang the last song. All was over.

*Anthropologist William Duncan Strong, who studied the Cahuilla in the 1920s.*

Just as it had been important to Mukat's creatures to mark his death, it was important to the Cahuillas to use rituals to mark death and all the important stages of life. Starting from birth, a Cahuilla went through several important changes: being officially named at around age 5, becoming initiated as a young adult around age 12 or 13, getting married later during his or her teens, and dying. Each of these events was marked by a ritual that announced the person was undergoing some change. For example, a teenaged boy

would be publicly recognized as a man after his initiation ritual. The rituals helped all the participants make the necessary changes to enter the next stage in their lives. A ceremony included the performance of a series of traditional actions in a certain order, helping the person leave the old status (such as boyhood) and to learn and accept some of the ways of the new status (such as manhood).

Birth, of course, is the start of the life cycle. When a Cahuilla child was born, the mother and infant went through a ceremony that lasted several days. The ritual was sponsored by the baby's father and his family, the mother's family, and the lineage leaders. They provided the food, herbs, and guidance needed for the ceremony. The birth ritual helped to emphasize the child's relationship with its lineage, as someone who needed care but was a part of the group.

Immediately after a child was born, it was bathed. The baby's relatives placed the mother and child in a pit kept warm by hot stones and sand. Herbs were placed in the pit for medicinal and religious purposes. Both the baby and the mother drank special herbal potions, and the mother was forbidden to eat salt and meat. In the meantime, lineage members went to the ceremonial house with guests, especially members of related families and friends from other communities. They brought gifts for the baby's family, and in turn the family gave food and valuables to their guests. People usually started saving food and making gift items such as baskets and strings of shell beads when they knew a woman was pregnant because it took a long time to save enough goods for the ceremonies. Then, when the ritual finally took place, both the hosts and the guests were able to fulfill their gift-giving obligations.

The baby did not receive an official name at birth. It would be called by nicknames until several children in the lineage reached age four or five, when the lineage would hold a naming ceremony for all of them. The net announced the time of the ritual. A huge group, including the local lineage and people from the families of the children's mothers, traveled a great distance to be at the ceremonial house on that day. The children's families gave gifts to all the guests. If the families had not saved up enough food for all these people, then the ritual would be postponed. As a result, some children were not named until age 9 or 10.

The net chose the children's names. The names were usually those of dead ancestors, and a name could not be used if it already belonged to a living person. W. D. Strong observed a naming ceremony, and he said that at about midnight, after a night of singing and dancing, the net would start naming the children. He would pick up a little boy or girl, hold the child up high, and dance slowly in the middle of the ceremonial house and the circled guests. Suddenly, he would shout the name

*Buckwheat, one of the many plants used by the Cahuilla to make herbal remedies.*

three times. Everyone repeated the name, sometimes exclaiming "Oh! ho-ho!" first. Sometimes the name first announced by the net was not the real name being given to a child. It might be a kind of decoy name, in case enemies or evil spirits were listening in order to learn a child's name to use in witchcraft against the youngster. In that case, the real name was bestowed upon the child in secret. Girls were often given names associated with flowers, plants, or household goods, such as the Cahuilla terms for "dried berry flour,"

*From jimsonweed the Cahuilla made a hallu-cinogenic drink that was sometimes given to boys at initiation ceremonies.*

"aprons," and "acorns on a cord." Boys were given names associated with birds, insects, or hunting, such as "centipede humps" and "marksman with a bow." These names gave each child a firm and unique identity.

The next important change in a young Cahuilla's status came at the time of adolescence, around age 12 or 13. Initiation ceremonies marked the young person's transition from childhood to a more adult status, with some of the responsibilities of full adults. Unlike the naming ritual, in which boys and girls were named together, initia-tions were held separately for boys and girls. All of a lineage's boys of appropriate age were initiated together. Girls were initiated individually.

The boys' initiation ritual could not begin until there was a great surplus of food. For months before the ceremony, hosts and guests saved food and prepared gifts for the feast. Meanwhile, the older men of the lineage instructed the adolescent boys (and sometimes the younger boys at the same time) in preparation for the initiation ceremony. They taught the boys their lineage history, songs belonging to their own clan, some "enemy" songs, and their obligations toward society.

For several days or even weeks, the boys were taken away in the daytime as a group to a private place to learn these things. The older men dramatized the lessons and put the boys under physical and mental pressure. The initiates were forced to run for long distances, kept awake for long periods, and taught dances and songs for hours on end. These strenuous physical activities and tests of bravery and resistance to pain led to a high degree of psychological stress that had the effect of inducing rapid and effective learning. The men made sand paintings with crushed colored earths, drawing designs that symbolized the Cahuilla concept of the universe. The men tattooed the boys and pierced their ears and nose so they could wear traditional ornaments. Some clans gave all or some of the boys a drink, toloache, made from *Datura in-*

*oxidia*, a hallucinogenic potatolike plant, so they would have visions of supernatural beings. Preparations of this plant, a variety of jimson weed, were widely used in ceremonies and as a painkiller. The boys were also given native tobacco (*nicoteana atlenuata*), a sedative, to smoke. As adults, they would pay their respects to the creative power by smoking on all ceremonial occasions.

Each night the boys returned to the ceremonial house or a sacred place, where each one sang three or four songs in turn, shaking rattles in accompaniment. The paxaa? was in charge of all the boys during these evenings. He carried a quiver made of deer, mountain sheep, or wildcat hide painted with designs in red and black.

The boys could not eat at all for a time, and then only a light meal of seeds and porridge. They wore "hunger belts" of twisted grass around their waists. They were observed carefully throughout their rigorous schedule of activities. Their dreams were used to indicate their talents and predict their future careers. The older men looked for boys who demonstrated special skills such as hunting ability, dancing and singing talent, and those whose dreams showed they had the potential to become shamans. If they recognized any of these abilities in a young man, they would later guide him to fulfill his potential in a special role by explaining the rules and regulations of that occupation.

*A ceremonial rattle made from turtle shells, sketched by Edward H. Davis in 1917.*

Finally, after enough food had been prepared and the boys had learned all they needed to know, the three-day ceremony, including great feasting, was held. Most members of the boys' lineage were there, along with people from the lineages of the boys' mothers. Guests and hosts exchanged gifts of food and valuables. The lineages' ceremonial leaders told the people that the boys were now men, and shamans blessed the event.

The girls' initiation was quite different. Each girl was initiated individually after she menstruated for the first time. A pit was dug for her in the earth in the center of the ceremonial house or near her home, similar to the one a woman and her newborn baby stayed in. The men lit a fire in the pit to heat it. When the pit was hot, they raked the fire out and lined the warm earth with grasses and herbs. The girl was placed in the pit and covered with more grass, furs, and hot sand. She had to stay in the pit for up to four or five days; the only time she could come out was when the pit needed to be reheated.

During the day, a haunik taught the girl her clan songs. Other people danced around the pit, chanting or singing. The girl's grandmother helped to teach the girl her proper role as an adult woman, food producer, and childbearer. The girl wore a hunger belt just like the ones the boys wore, but she did not have to fast. However, she drank an herb potion and a light gruel. She could not eat food with salt in it.

She was not allowed to scratch her head with her bare fingers—in some clans, people believed this action would cause a lifelong problem with dandruff and hair loss—so she used a wooden scratcher if her head felt itchy. These rules established a sense of discipline in the girl.

Sometimes one or several girls would be initiated at the same time as several boys. On the last morning of the ceremony, when the boys and girls had all learned the songs, they could wash. Among some clans, they were then painted all over their arms and faces with dots of red, black, and white. The girls painted symbols on rocks, and there are still faintly visible red designs apparently symbolic of puberty seen on some rocks in the Cahuilla area. The paints were made of crushed colored earths and minerals mixed with animal fat or egg white. After going through an initiation ceremony, a young man or woman was considered marriageable.

Soon after young people were initiated, their parents might arrange a marriage for them. Girls were usually married at the age of 12 or 13, whereas boys were more likely to marry at 17 or 18, or older. Marriage caused a change in a person's life. Suddenly, he or she would be responsible for providing food for a new family unit; the young man would even have to find meat for his new wife's relatives. For the young woman, marriage caused a change in residence as well as responsibility, because she left her own lineage community to go live in the lineage community of her husband.

When a union was arranged, the families involved held a ceremony. The boy's family presented a large gift of food and valuables to the girl's family. Then the girl was brought to the ceremonial house in the boy's community. There they had a feast for the boy's family and several of the girl's relatives. After the feast, one of the boy's relatives talked to the couple. He told the boy to hunt game for the girl and her parents. He told the girl to provide for her husband by gathering and preparing enough food for him. He warned them both not to argue. Everyone who had come for the feast heard the talk of the boy's relative. When it was finished, the bride and groom were officially married.

If the girl was still too young to become a wife, perhaps 11 or younger, she was brought to the boy's home and raised by her future mother-in-law. When she reached the marriageable age of 12 or 13, she would actually marry the boy, as long as his family still felt she would make a good wife. The young couple lived with the boy's parents until they had children. Then they moved to their own home nearby. If the girl and boy were old enough to be married when the marriage arrangement was made, they simply went through the marriage ceremony and then moved to their own home. But the marriage was never considered complete until the couple had children.

When a person died, a whole series of rituals was performed to mark the end of the life cycle. Immediately after a death occurred, the person was cremated in a large fire, along with his or her house and possessions. The Cahuillas believed that destroying the pos-

*Copy of a pictograph from southern California. The designs were painted in red. They are believed to have been made during a Cahuilla girl's initiation ceremony.*

# ROCK ART

Cahuillas painted, incised, and pecked pictures on large rocks throughout their territory. These pictures, called pictographs or petroglyphs, were used mainly in religious contexts, though they occasionally served to record historical events.

Pictographs were painted designs. The Cahuillas made their paints from minerals, using limonite to get white paint, magnetite or charcoal to get black, and hematite to get red. They mixed the crushed minerals with melted animal fat or egg whites to make them stick to rocks and last through harsh weather. They used paint brushes made from yucca fiber.

Petroglyphs were designs cut into a rock face using a much harder stone or pecked out slowly using a large stone to chip off tiny pieces from the rock.

There were a wide variety of designs—humanlike figures, concentric circles, mazelike patterns, crosshatching, and parallel vertical lines. The precise uses and meanings of each design were known only to a few priests and shamans. These meanings and uses are now a forgotten part of the Cahuillas' sacred history. But on many rocks in what used to be Cahuilla territory the rock art remains, a reminder of how much has been lost over the years since the last religious leaders practiced there.

*A drawing of an early 19th-century petroglyph. The design is believed to show the first encounter between Indians and non-Indians.*

sessions made it possible for the dead person to use them in the afterlife. The remaining members of the houschold built another home nearby. Relatives and neighbors came to the cremation and gave gifts to the net; any other net who heard of the death might send valuable shells, a kind of money, to the net of the dead person's lineage to honor the deceased and his or her relatives.

Another ritual was usually held within a month of the cremation; the immediate family, the lineage, and all those who had attended the cremation came to this ceremony. Women of the dead person's lineage dragged animal skins and pieces of shrubbery around the floor of the ceremonial house to erase the tracks of the dead person; this would prevent the return of the person's soul. During the night the people sang songs to honor the deceased person and help his or her soul leave this world and go into the afterlife. There were different songs depending on whether the deceased was male or female. After midnight, the dead person's family threw food and baskets, which the guests gathered up to take home. A period of mourning also marked the death; women who were close relatives cut their hair to show mourning.

Every year or two, several clans would join to hold a *nukil* ceremony to honor all members who had died since the last nukil. A nukil ended the period of mourning. This ceremony usually took place in winter, and only when the host lineage had stored up enough food and gifts for the guests from other lineages. This was the most elaborate and significant ceremony of the Cahuillas, one that could involve several hundred people. Clans from both the Wildcat and Coyote sides of society participated in the nukil, so gathering up enough food was a large task. Preparations started immediately after the net and other lineage leaders met in council to decide on the correct time to hold the ritual, several months in advance. Then every member of the community started getting ready; each family was required to contribute food and gifts, as well as to make housing and entertainment arrangements for the guests.

The people also knew the nukil would present a great chance for trading, because so many people would be there, so the women started making baskets, and the men started stringing shell beads and making nets, bows and arrows, and other goods. In fact, the nukil ceremony was very important not only as a way of marking a life change but also because of this trading and the opportunity it presented to arrange marriages and work out disputes with other lineages. Families looked forward to the ritual, and they discussed which singers should perform, which songs the deceased would enjoy hearing, which lineages should be invited, and all the other arrangements.

Invitations to the ceremony were given by the net of the host lineage; he would send a string of shell beads to the net of any invited lineage. If the

*The Cahuillas' traditional burial practice of cremating the body and burning the home and possessions of a deceased member, sketched by Edward H. Davis in 1917.*

other net accepted the beads, that meant his lineage would attend and participate.

The ceremony lasted for seven days and nights. The first three days were spent in dancing and in making additional preparations to ensure the success of the entire ritual. The association of shamans performed a series of dances in the ceremonial house to "clear the atmosphere" of evil spirits or ghosts and to purify the minds of any humans or supernaturals who might have evil intentions. At the same time, many other people went on a big rabbit and deer hunt to make sure there would be plenty of meat for all the guests.

The last four days of the nukil were used for a continuous cycle of songs performed by special ritual singers from many of the lineages present. The songs told a story that described the Cahuilla concept of the universe and established the role of the Cahuilla people in it. This was done through the story of the death of the creator Mukat and the first funeral and nukil ceremonies held for him.

The very first song was about the ironwood used to burn the dead. At the end of this and all the other songs, everyone present exclaimed "hum-hum-uh!" three times and then exhaled up into the air. This blew away the spirits and helped them go up to the afterlife. Each song was many minutes long, and there were long pauses between songs, so the ritual singing went on all through the night. Each song narrated a small episode in the story of the creation of the world and finally Mukat's death. These songs continued every night during the rest of the ceremony.

After the singing ended on the last night, gifts of food and other valuables were divided among all the guests. Then images of everyone who had died since the last nukil, made out of wood, grass, fur, beads, and other materials by the older people, were brought out and placed on the ground in front of the ceremonial house. The net prayed over them, and then the images were burned. After the nukil was over, the period of mourning also ended and gifts were presented to all the guests who had attended.

These elaborate funeral ceremonies helped the souls of the dead get to the afterlife safely. But before they arrived in the afterlife, the souls appeared to the living in many forms. Sometimes the souls actually appeared as some object or being, but usually they showed up in dreams or were felt as cold drafts or odors. Often, the souls asked living people to join them so they would not be lonely. Sometimes a soul could not make it to the afterlife, and it lived on forever, feeling homeless and anxious. But if enough people came to the funeral ceremonies and performed the rituals correctly, the soul had a good chance of getting to the afterlife. Like the other rituals of the Cahuilla, the death rituals marked an important change in the cycle of life, from birth to death and the afterlife. ▲

A Desert Cahuilla Woman, *photographed by Edward S. Curtis in 1924.*

# 5

# THE
# ARRIVAL
# OF
# EUROPEANS

The Cahuillas did not live in an isolated world. They were familiar with people from many other cultures. They traded and shared many goods with people from all of the neighboring Indian nations, such as the Serranos to the north, the Diegueños to the south, and the Gabrielinos and Luiseños to the west, on the coast. They also intermarried with these groups. They formed military and economic alliances with some neighboring groups, such as the Serranos, Gabrielinos, Luiseños, and Halchidhoma, to battle with other tribes, such as the Yuma (Quechans) to the east. So it is not surprising that they heard from other Indians about European people before they ever saw them. When the Europeans finally did begin to interact regularly with the Cahuillas, they introduced them to some beliefs, material goods, and ways of life that began changing traditional Cahuilla customs.

In the late 18th century, Spain began to colonize California in order to prevent other European nations, such as Great Britain and Russia, from acquiring the area. An important part of col-

onization was the government's effort to convert all California Indians to Catholicism. Spain had ruled Mexico since 1521. Spanish priests came into the southern California area from Mexico along with troops and in a few years set up Catholic missions along the California coast. The first was Mission San Diego, established in 1769. The priests at these missions used persuasion and military force to impose Catholicism and Spanish cultural traditions on the Indians.

The first Europeans to meet with the Cahuillas were a group of Spaniards who came to their territory in the company of Indians from Mexico, under the direction of Juan Bautista de Anza. In 1774 Anza and his men set out to look for a good, easily passable land route between the state of Sonora in Mexico and the Monterey Peninsula of California, where one of the earliest missions had been established. Monterey, a Spanish administrative center, had a large military and civilian community. The people there needed supplies from Mexico, especially European manufac-

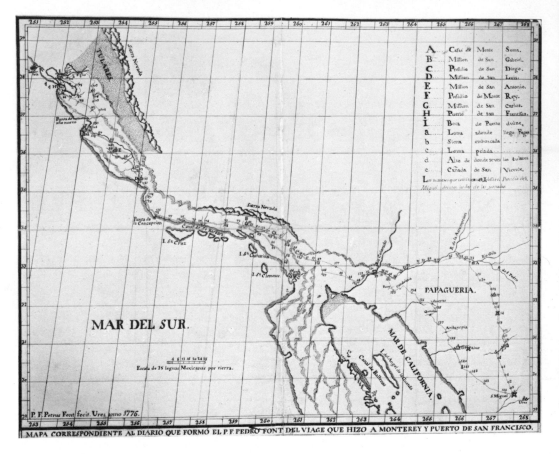

MAPA CORRESPONDIENTE AL DIARIO QUE FORMÓ EL P.F PEDRO FONT DEL VIAGE QUE HIZO A MONTEREY Y PUERTO DE SAN FRANCISCO.

*A map showing the route of Juan Bautista de Anza's 1774 expedition from Mexico to the California coast, drawn two years later and based on a diary kept by a member of the expedition. The route between the Sierra Nevada mountain range and the Pacific Ocean is marked by numbers corresponding to the days of the journey.*

tured goods that were not available in California. Because it took months to go by sea from Mexico to Monterey and storms made travel by sea hazardous, the colonists in Monterey hoped that an efficient land route could be discovered.

While searching for this land route, Anza and his men passed through the territory of the Wiastum Cahuilla clan without asking permission. In defense of their territory, the Cahuillas shot at the intruders. Other Indians, especially the Yumas on the Colorado River, also attacked the Spaniards in 1781 for invading their territory and damaging their crops. The Yumas killed a priest and other Spaniards, and forced the invaders to retreat. With the land route Anza had discovered now unusable, the Spanish government was forced to continue sending people and supplies by ship along the coast of colonial California. With only a sea route open, colonization and the construction of missions had to continue along the California coastline, where supplies could reach the colonists.

Because the Cahuilla's communities were so far inland, where there were no Spanish outposts, the Cahuilla at first had little contact with Spanish soldiers, civilians, and priests. They began to hear of mission life from other Indians who lived closer to the coast and to missions such as San Gabriel, San Luis Rey, and San Diego. In the early 1800s some Cahuillas visited these Spanish settlements, and a few stayed long enough to learn about Christianity and European ways. There are mission records showing that some Cahuillas were baptized as early as 1809. In addition, the Cahuillas began to hear about and occasionally to see new material goods brought by the priests, including pack horses, cattle, glass beads, woven cloth, china plates, and metal tools. They also learned about many technological processes previously unknown to them, such as soapmaking and ironworking.

The Spaniards also brought diseases, which were particularly damaging. Some of the European diseases, such as smallpox and measles, had never occurred before in the Americas, and the Indians had no immunity to them. As these diseases spread, devastating population losses were suffered among all native Californians, including the Cahuillas.

By 1819 many missions had been established along the coast. From them the Church reached out to the nearer inland Indians, but not as far as the Col-

*The Spanish mission of San Gabriel Arcangel near the southern California coast, painted in 1832. An Indian dwelling is in the foreground at right.*

orado River, which was the home of hostile tribes. The Church set up several mission outposts near Cahuilla territory at San Bernardino, Santa Ysabel, and Pala. Because a few Cahuillas were already practicing Catholicism and even speaking a little Spanish, some of them now received the Spaniards more warmly than they had at first. They adopted some European customs and traded for Spanish merchandise. They began to wear European-style clothing (dresses for women, trousers and shirts for men), to speak Spanish, to farm in the European manner, to use horses for farming, transport, and herding, and to raise cattle. More of them began to practice Catholicism. The military force associated with the mission outposts helped to enforce the religious lessons of the priests. The missions also provided a place for teaching the Indians such practical European crafts as brick-making and woodworking.

All the missions established ranches to care for the increasingly larger herds of cattle, offspring of the few cattle originally brought by the Spaniards to ensure a reliable source of meat. Along with the cattle, the Spaniards had brought with them horses and several new types of plants, such as fruits, oats, and wheat. The priests often forcibly detained Indians at mission-run ranches and farms to use them as laborers. By working for the Spaniards, the Cahuillas soon became skilled at cattle raising, agriculture, and crafts. But although Cahuillas were using European ranching and farming techniques when they worked for the Spanish missions, they continued to use their traditional skills to support themselves. They depended on their wage-paying jobs to supplement, rather than replace, the foods they acquired through traditional methods of harvesting wild plants and hunting game.

Despite all the changes brought by the influence of the Spanish priests, the Cahuilla remained politically and economically independent. They did not ask Spanish people to lead them or make decisions for them, and they could have survived without Spanish goods or money.

Spain continued to control the California coast until 1822. In that year, the Mexican Revolution, which had started in 1810, finally succeeded in driving the Spanish forces out of Mexico and also California. From this time on, governors of California were appointed by the Mexican government and were men who had been born in North America rather than Spain. This change in power brought about a new period of land exploitation by Mexicans in the California interior. Exploration continued and there was increased use of the land, including Cahuilla lands, for agriculture and ranching. The Mexicans renewed the push for exploration; they sent Captain José Romero to find a route from California to Arizona and back down to Mexico. Romero and his men, following a route used by Indians,

*San Gabriel Mission in the middle of the 19th century. The missions often maintained large herds of cattle to provide their residents with a reliable source of meat.*

went directly through Cahuilla territory, stopping in the Cahuilla area now known as Palm Springs, which they called *Agua Caliente* (hot water) to obtain water.

After its victory, the Mexican government had begun taking land away from the Spanish missions and giving out parcels to its own people. Although the Mexicans did not choose to settle in most of Cahuilla territory, they did start ranches in a few of the valleys on Cahuilla land. Gradually the Cahuillas began to find work as skilled laborers on these ranches. The Mexican ranchers relied completely on the Indians to provide ranch management and labor.

One of these new Mexican landowners was Antonio María Lugo. He and his sons had a good relationship with the Cahuilla Indians who lived nearby in the San Bernardino area. Some of the Cahuillas worked for Lugo. In 1846, five Cahuilla clans, which were united under the leadership of a Cahuilla clan leader named Juan Antonio, moved closer to the Lugo land. Their purpose was to help the Lugos protect their 37,000 acres from bands of Ute Indians from the north, who stole horses and cattle from ranchers and the Cahuilla. In this they were protecting their own interests as well because they would gain some power in dealings with the Mexican ranchers.

Like Juan Antonio, several other traditional clan and community leaders continued to serve as political leaders during this time of change. These leaders functioned as diplomats to ease re-

*(continued on page 88)*

# THE HOT SPRINGS
# MEDICINE PLACE

*Agua Caliente became well known and eventually popular as a health resort. Cahuillas had long recognized the healing powers of the hot springs, as shown in a story told by Francisco Patencio.*

Now Sungrey [one of the nukatem] came through and made this spring a medicine place to cure himself and left it to cure sickness in other people for always. He knew that a giant blue frog, a red racer snake, a bear, a mountain lion, and a little child with fair skin were living there, and he opened up the way for them to live in the spring. The medicine men [shamans] did not have the same power. Some had the power to cure one thing, and some another. When the medicine man belonging to the Fox Tribe felt that his power was not strong enough to cure himself, he prayed three days and nights. He asked his guardian spirit how he could cure himself to get well. The last night it was shown to him in a dream. He found that he was to go into the spring and see the spirits that were living there in it. The medicine man went to the spring and entered into an open place like a den.

When the medicine man first went into the spring he did not see the water. He first saw the frog that was sitting in the doorway, and he spoke to the frog and told him that he was sick and had come to him to be cured. Then he lay down in front of the frog's door. The frog went around his body and showed him where to go next. The medicine man went and came to the snake. He lay down again and told the snake that he was sick and had come to be cured by him. The red racer snake coiled around his body and sent him to the bear. He lay down in front of the bear, and the bear opened his giant mouth and licked his body with his tongue. This he did three times. Then he told him to go to the mountain lion. The mountain lion was sitting down, and the medicine man lay down at his feet and told him he was sick and had come to be cured by him. The mountain lion did the same as the bear. The child was the spirit of the chief power among them, and lived somewhat apart. The mountain lion sent him on to the child.

Now the child had taken the form of an old man, and was sitting smoking a pipe. The medicine man went in and lay down before him. He told him that he was sick and had come to be cured. But the old man was looking away and did not look at or speak to him. So the medicine man said again, "I am sick and came down to be cured." Then he rose and reached for the old man's pipe, which the old man handed to him quickly. The medicine man swallowed the smoke three times. Then the old man snatched it away. The medicine man then felt more power and knew that he was cured.

He then started to go back, but as he looked up the way seemed so far he thought he could never get out. He saw a little stream of water coming in from the mountain, forming a small pool in the shape of a cup, then rising to the top of the ground. The medicine man stepped into this stream, and the water lifted him quickly to the top. Then he was a well man again, and had more power to cure his people than ever before.

*A bathhouse at Agua Caliente, near Palm Springs, California, in the early 20th century. Some Cahuillas were employed in the baths, which attracted non-Indians who sought the healing effects of the hot springs.*

*The Lugo family ranch house, photographed around 1885.*

(*continued from page 85*)

lations between their people and the Mexicans and Europeans. Antonio Garra was another leader who tried to protect his own people's interests along with the interests of the Mexican and Spanish settlers of California. In the 1840s, they began their struggle against the U.S. government, which had started military action to take over California. Juan Antonio and his men also defended California against the U.S. invasion. They accompanied one of Lugo's sons in pursuit of a group of Luiseño Indians allied with the United States. Lugo and Juan Antonio's Cahuillas fought well, and many Luiseños were killed. Others, taken prisoner and put in Juan Antonio's custody, were later killed as well.

Despite the combined efforts of Mexicans and some Cahuillas and other Indian peoples, the U.S. forces won. The United States gained control of Cal-

ifornia even before winning the Mexican War in 1848. In the same year, gold was discovered in California. Now the Cahuilla lands would be exploited more than ever before. Americans passed through the area in increasing numbers on their way to the gold fields. They also flooded into the area to take up ranching and farming, often taking choice hunting and food-gathering lands, especially areas with good water resources, away from the Cahuillas for their own use. Many Cahuilla communities became frequent stopover places for Mexican, European, and American travelers and later became stagecoach and mail stops as well.

By the early 1850s, the relationship between California Indians and non-Indians had become strained. The non-Indians viewed Cahuilla territory as desirable land, and conflicts arose over who had the right to own and use this land. Often, the non-Indians moved into fields prepared by Cahuillas and simply took them over. They also used springs and streams that belonged to the Cahuillas, a particularly objectionable form of trespassing in such an arid area.

Cahuillas were able to earn money by charging for the use of the springs on their land, their labor, and by growing foods for visitors. In addition, they worked for the Americans on ranches and in the fruit industry. They also made money in their own enterprises and continued to support themselves with traditional hunting and gathering.

Juan Antonio continued to assert his right to leadership within his territory, in an effort to maintain the political autonomy of his people. In 1851, José del Carmen Lugo asked Juan Antonio and his men to follow a non-Indian outlaw band. Armed with revolvers, the outlaws had been terrorizing people throughout southern California. Juan Antonio's forces, using only bows and arrows, managed to kill all but one of the outlaws. There was an investigation and a hearing in Los Angeles. The American court determined that the killings were justified, and the Cahuillas were rewarded with $100 worth of supplies.

By the mid-1850s, however, amid growing tensions, after many years of supporting the Lugos and other non-Indians, some Cahuillas allied with Colorado River Indians to fight against non-Indian intruders. This effort ended when Antonio Garra, another Cahuilla clan leader who headed the defenders, was captured and killed.

In 1862 and 1863, a smallpox epidemic killed many Cahuillas. The Cahuilla population, which may have been as high as 6,000 to 10,000 people before contact with the Europeans, was devastated—only about 2,500 were left. Many knowledgeable and wise leaders, including Juan Antonio, had died and

*Cattle ranchers on Morongo Reservation demonstrate their skills at a tribal roundup in 1968.*

*Francisco and Dolores Patencio, who carried the knowledge of traditional skills and stories into the 20th century, photographed in 1928.*

the people could no longer make a strong stand against outsiders. The reduced population was left in a weak position in relation to non-Indians, whose population in the area was growing rapidly. Yet, in order to live, many of the young people had to continue to work for non-Indian farmers, ranchers, miners, and lumber companies, despite the epidemic and the erosion of good faith between Indians and non-Indians.

Some of these young Indians learned new skills, including reading and writing, from the Americans and Europeans. Francisco Patencio, the man who recounted many of the legends in this book, learned how to read and write when he lived with an American family called the Crafts. In his 1943 book, he recalls learning to read and write English in the 1860s.

No, I never went to school a day in my life. I began to learn to read and write Spanish. That was not so hard, for I had spoken that all my life. But the English. That was hard. I have never stopped studying English. When I became old enough to think my own thoughts, I knew that the time of the bows and arrows and guns was gone. Now it was paper with the names written, that my people had to do. I thought it would be a good thing to know what the names and the sign marks of my people meant when they were put on paper. This was a good thing for me to know.

I know about all the Treaties from the time of the Missions and Spanish Grants. All the agreements since Spain, Mexico, and United States have taken the land. After I had read about the Spanish and Mexican treaties, I wanted to understand about the American agreements. That is how I came to study by myself to read and write English. I read and write English, Spanish, French, and speak seven Indian dialects.

Such excellent language skills were not unusual for the Cahuillas who acted as leaders for their people.

By the 1870s, some non-Indians were beginning to realize that the Cahuillas and other Indians would not be able to support themselves if the theft of their land and water continued. Some important Indian advocate groups, such as the Indian Rights Association, were formed at this time. To help resolve the conflicts between Indians and non-Indians in southern California, these advocates recommended reserving some land strictly for the Indians. This idea was accepted by some because it seemed to offer needed protection for Cahuillas and other Indians. It was more selfishly welcomed by others who were themselves settling in southern California because it meant they could take their pick of nonreserved lands.

From 1875 through 1877, the administration of President Ulysses S. Grant established the first reservations for Cahuilla people. These included the Cahuilla, Torres-Martinez, Cabazon, and Morongo reservations. The reservations were managed by the Bureau of Indian Affairs (BIA), an agency of the Department of the Interior. The location of these reservations had been recommended by Indian agents appointed by Grant's administration to protect the native population of southern California. But these reservations were not very well protected by the law. Many settlers who wanted to use reservation

*Cabezon, a 19th-century Cahuilla leader, for whom Cabazon reservation was named.*

land for themselves sued the government to see if the courts would really uphold the executive orders by which President Grant had established the reservations. Because descriptions of reservation boundaries were often vague in these executive orders, and because Indians at the time had no civil rights, it was easy for settlers to take much of the land.

In the early 1880s, so many Cahuillas and other southern California Indians were being pushed off their land that the U.S. Congress established a commission to investigate the situation. Congress had been pressured into forming the Mission Indian Commission (more commonly known as the Smiley Commission) by the Indian advocacy groups. Many of the people who worked on behalf of the Cahuilla at this time had become aware of the Indians of southern California by reading two books by Helen Hunt Jackson. Several years earlier, Jackson had been in-censed at learning of the extreme losses of Indian land to settlers. After extensive research, she had written *A Century of Dishonor* (1881), a work of nonfiction showing that the U.S. government had broken promises made to Indians in treaties. As a member of the Smiley Commission, Jackson came to feel that only a work of fiction could communicate the human dimensions of the losses being suffered by the Indians. Her novel *Ramona* told of a southern California Indian who was wrongly and cruelly killed by a non-Indian settler. It caught the public's attention and even-

*The Cahuilla woman whose experiences inspired Helen Hunt Jackson to write her 1884 novel,* Ramona.

tually helped the Cahuillas and other southern California Indians.

On January 12, 1891, Congress passed the Act for the Relief of Mission Indians, which formally established reservations for the Indians of southern California. The reservation boundaries were based on the recommendations of the Smiley Commission. While setting up reservations and defining boundaries, this congressional act actually took land away from several reservations. Reservation lands were held in trust by the U.S. government for the Indians, and no property taxes ever had to be paid on these lands. After the reservation act went into effect, the Cahuillas were left with only two-thirds of the land they had controlled prior to 1891. In the meantime, the Dawes Act of 1887 allowed the division of reservation land into separate tracts that were to be given (allotted) to individual Indians. Efforts at allotment on Cahuilla reservations brought about conflicts that went on for many years.

Reservation life changed Cahuilla traditions more than their first contact with people from Spain and Mexico had. These changes resulted from the belief of many non-Indians, and especially the Indian agents, that Indian people should be assisted economically but that Indian culture should be destroyed because it was the complete opposite of what they saw as "civilization." They did not see the Cahuillas as people who had been ingenious enough to discover an effective way to live in what seemed like a very barren area. Rather, they saw that the Cahuillas ate foods, lived in houses, and had religious practices that were noticeably different from those of Europeans and Americans.

The advocate groups and Indian agents decided to try to change Indian culture by starting with the children, who had not yet had a chance to learn all the important aspects of their traditions. Every Cahuilla child, like American Indian children across the entire United States, was to be taught English and kept from speaking his or her own language. The Americans sent the children to U.S. government schools, where they learned to speak English and perform various trades. Schools beyond the elementary level were located in only a few places across the country, so children were forced to leave their families behind to attend these schools.

Furthermore, the Americans felt they could teach the Cahuillas to give up their lineage communities by giving each family an allotment of land for its own individual farm. Finally, they banned traditional Indian religions and subjected the Cahuillas to religious persecution. For example, Indian agents tried to keep people from attending their accustomed ceremonies. For the second time in a little more than a hundred years, considerable effort was put into Christianizing Cahuillas and other Indians.

On the reservations, some Cahuillas lived off their land using Euro-American techniques more than traditional ones. Traditional hunting and harvesting techniques were no longer sufficient to feed people, especially because the cattle introduced by the Spanish had eaten many of the plant foods used by Cahuillas and the game animals they hunted, thereby reducing natural food resources. Cahuillas became more reliant on farming, cattle ranching, land rentals, wage labor, and employment on the reservations by the BIA. They occasionally earned money by acting in movies or doing other odd jobs.

The Indian Service representatives, who often lived right on reservation land, controlled much of reservation life, especially the political structure. The agents appointed judges, captains, and police. The Cahuillas and other Indians on reservations actively objected to being controlled in this way, partly by forming protest groups, such as the Mission Indian Federation. In 1934 Congress passed the Indian Reorganization Act (IRA), which allowed people on reservations more responsibility for managing their own affairs. Until that time, most Indians in the United States had been deprived by law of the right to manage their own affairs. Now they could elect their own leaders and make binding decisions about such things as use of their own land and their economic development. Because their land had been held in trust by the government, they could neither sell it nor borrow money by mortgaging it. Under the IRA, they were able to start businesses.

They also could borrow money from banks, private individuals, or government agencies. Some Cahuillas used this money to build homes, buy cattle, horses, and equipment, and buy back their traditional lands.

Many Cahuillas protested the land allotment program. Even before the 1920s, many had been upset because they had not received the individual allotments of land promised them by the federal government. However, most of these allotments would have been too small for efficient farming. Cahuillas had to continue to rely on wage labor and other means of earning money.

A special situation arose in the Palm Springs area because the Agua Caliente Indian Reservation occupied half of the city's land. After much pressure and even lawsuits brought by Cahuillas, Congress passed the Equalization Law of 1959. This act made sure that all entitled individuals from the Agua Caliente reservation would receive land parcels of equal value.

In the 1930s, Cahuillas were as affected as other Americans by the Great Depression. Many who had been employed elsewhere returned to reservation lands where they could live with less expense. They practiced small-scale farming and had the added advantage of being able to return to traditional hunting and gathering practices, which alleviated some of the economic stresses of the depression.

Many Cahuilla men volunteered to serve in the armed forced during the

*A store near Palm Springs, California, in 1939. The Indian Reorganization Act of 1934 enabled Indians to borrow money, buy land, and set up businesses. The Indian owner of this plot of land leased it to the non-Indian store owner.*

Second World War. Some returned with bitterness, expecting economic and other improvements, which did not take place. Shamans used traditional medicine to help those who were under psychological stress as a result of their wartime experiences. A few of the ex-GIs took advantage of the GI Bill, taking out low-cost loans to start their own businesses.

Although matters did not really improve in the area of land ownership and income earning, they did improve in the areas of health, education, and welfare. This is partly because, after World War II, there was less federal supervision of California Indians. Suddenly Cahuillas had to take more control of these issues. They also gained access to some new programs financed by the federal and state governments in the 1960s, especially the War on Poverty programs initiated during the administration of President Lyndon Johnson. These were attempts to increase job opportunities, access to health care, and the quality of education for low-income people throughout the nation. Being given back some control over their lives gave the Cahuillas a chance to find a workable blend between their traditional culture and the new technologies and beliefs held by the modern Western world. ▲

*Joe Lomas, a Cahuilla singer and storyteller, photographed about 1968.*

6

# THE
# CAHUILLA
# TODAY

Today most Cahuillas still live in the same general area their ancestors inhabited for thousands of years. They do not, however, own their traditional clan lands. Instead, they live on the reservations that were set aside for them and other Indian people of southern California by the U.S. government during the 1800s. They own the reservation lands as corporate groups, and some own land as individuals. The reservations of Morongo, Santa Rosa, Cahuilla, Cabazon, Soboba, Torres-Martinez, and Los Coyotes, where most of the Cahuillas live, are all located in rural areas. The continued importance of family relationships, some aspects of traditional culture, and the attractions of rural life—including open space, fresh air, and lots of opportunity for outdoor recreational activities—keep most of the young people on the reservations even though economic opportunities are not abundant there. These reservations exist near cities such as Banning and Indio, or rural communities inhabited mainly by non-Indians. A large part of the Agua Caliente Reservation is within the city limits of Palm Springs.

On the reservations, many of the same plants known to the ancient Cahuilla still grow and are used in traditional ways by modern Cahuillas, both for food and as medicine. Acorns and cactus buds are still eaten with great enjoyment. Wild animals are less abundant but are also still used in some of the traditional ways. Deer and quail, for example, are two traditional dishes sometimes found on the family table. However, other animals that formerly provided meat, especially mountain sheep and pronghorn, cannot be hunted because they are now near extinction due to the encroachment of modern settlements. But the plant and animal life is no longer as abundant as before, and the reservation lands cover much less territory than their traditional lands. Although modern Cahuillas no longer live by hunting game and harvesting wild plant foods, they remember and honor the ways of the ancient Cahuilla people, which lasted for some time after outsiders came to their area.

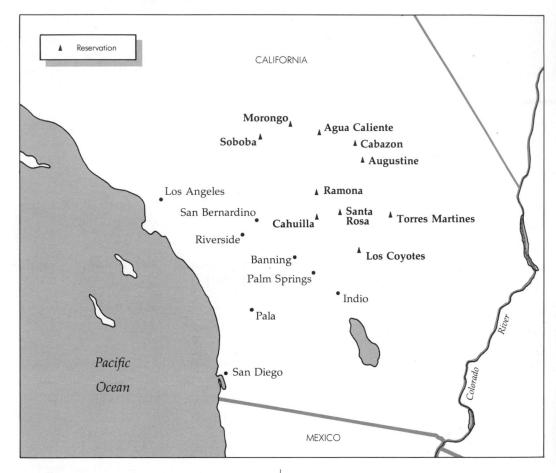

Largely as a result of marriages with people from other tribes, Cahuillas live and work side by side on the same reservations with other Indians, including the Chemehuevis, Luiseños, and Serranos. Homes are widely separated on the reservation so that the people can spread out and use the land to earn a living through farming and cattle ranching and by operating recreational facilities, harvesting timber, and leasing land for grazing, farming, and various businesses.

Some of the reservations run money-making businesses for the benefit of their members, including the public campground at Los Coyotes and tourist facilities at the beautiful canyons on Agua Caliente. Bingo halls run by the Cabazon and Morongo reservations provide employment for reservation residents, and some of the profits are used to support tribal administration and special projects.

Not all Cahuillas live on the reservations. Hundreds live in the California cities of Los Angeles, Riverside, Palm Springs, and San Diego. Others live on the East Coast or in foreign countries. During the last few years, scholarships from various sources have increased educational opportunities for Cahuillas, and urban Cahuillas now embark upon varied careers. Many graduate from high school and go on to college or trade school so that they can pursue employment as teachers, social workers, civil service employees (in government offices), health service providers, factory workers, secretaries, and construction workers, as well as in many other positions. But these city dwellers seldom abandon their ties to their traditional lands and the reservations. They return to the reservations to participate in religious ceremonies, visit relatives, spend a few peaceful days hunting, or enjoy the recreational possibilities of rural life. In fact, many of them retire to the reservation because it is where they prefer to be for cultural and social reasons. Here they can enjoy a life-style that is comfortable and less costly than they can find elsewhere.

Reservations are not run by the net or other traditional leaders. Instead, each reservation is run by a business committee as a separate political and economic unit. The committee members are elected by reservation residents every two or three years. Both men and women serve on these committees; recently, women have emerged as strong leaders in the formal political process, expanding their traditional roles as informal community leaders.

Many Cahuilla women are now serving as elected leaders in a society that was traditionally male-oriented. Over a long period of time, women achieved more equality and power in tribal affairs. This trend was first seen in the late 1890s when many men were away from home working at cash-paying jobs. Some women began to take on the management of important ceremonies, which they had not done before.

Women's involvement as cultural nurturers increased during and after the First and Second World Wars, when men were again away for long periods of time. Meanwhile, the Indian Reorganization Act had guaranteed to women voting rights on reservations. By the 1950s, many women were serving on tribal councils and today have responsibilities and opportunities equal to those of men for tribal as well as religious and family affairs.

Young people also are often elected and given the opportunity to act as leaders, although the traditional respect for older people (called elders) continues. The business committees manage the reservation with the assistance of subcommittees whose members they appoint. Staff members of the Bureau of Indian Affairs continue to work with people on the reservations in matters having to do with land. Economic issues are extremely important because the reservation land is often of poor quality for farming and far away from water sources. Reservations are usually distant from county services and job opportunities. Therefore, a vital function of the committees is to work out economic development programs for the reservations to help the residents find financial stability and to provide for water, power, health facilities, and emergency services. Some people, mostly in the Palm Springs area, however, own and manage land and businesses that are quite profitable. Although every reservation has its own government, they are not isolated from one another; many belong to countywide, statewide, or national Indian organizations that work to solve problems shared with other Indians and improve conditions for reservation Indians. They still attend ceremonies, fiestas, and sports events on other reservations, and marriages between people from different reservations are usual.

Cahuillas no longer live in traditional housing. During the past century, especially during the 1970s and 1980s, they have been building houses of various types. Cahuilla houses today often have brick or wooden siding and look just like those in many American communities. Adobe houses are still sometimes used. The furnishings inside the houses are similar to those in rural or suburban communities throughout the United States. There are electric appliances in the kitchen, store-bought chairs, beds, and chests in the living rooms and bedrooms. Cahuillas own radios, television sets, and videocassette recorders. Books fill shelves, and family photos as well as heirlooms of traditional culture are displayed. Networks of paved and dirt roads crisscross

the reservations, making them accessible to cars. Cahuilla people own cars or pickup trucks. However, many also own horses, which they use in ranching tasks and for recreational riding. As in most rural areas, health, emergency, and other centralized services exist on a small scale. Not all reservations have fire stations, police forces, or health centers; they use the services provided by local city, county, or state agencies. However, they do have some facilities that they share; for example, the Indian-run Morongo Indian Health Clinic serves people from nearby reservations. Each reservation also has a tribal hall for meetings, offices for committee members and other staff, a library, and one or more churches.

The Cahuilla today practice several different religions. Most are Catholics, but some are Protestants. Marriage and christening ceremonies are held in the church to which the family belongs. But most Cahuillas still practice at least some aspects of their traditional religion. People still call on the traditional concept of ?iva?a to explain natural phenomena. They believe disease, disaster, and death can be caused by supernatural retribution for wrongdoing. And modern life-cycle ceremonies use traditional practices, especially funerals and memorial services, which include customs directly related to the nukil ceremony. Family members and guests from all over come to participate in the rituals, and they perform the song cycles about the creation of the world and Mukat's death. However, because

# A CAHUILLA ELDER TODAY

Katherine Siva Saubel is a respected tribal elder who has been particularly successful at combining Cahuilla traditions and non-Indian ways. She was born on Los Coyotes Reservation in the early 20th century and remembers as a child traveling with her parents and her brothers and sisters in a wagon to visit relatives at various other reservations. They camped out in the open each night during their travels because it took several days to cover distances that today take only a few hours by car.

Mrs. Saubel now lives on Morongo Reservation, the home of her late husband, Mariano. She is widely respected by Cahuillas for her knowledge of their traditions and as a political leader. She has been chairperson of her tribe and a member of the Los Coyotes Tribal Council. Mrs. Saubel has been recognized many times by non-Indian as well as by Cahuilla institutions for her work in preserving the customs of the Cahuilla and explaining their traditions to non-Indians. She has served on the Native American Heritage Commission and the Riverside County Historical Commission, which honored her as its Historian of the Year for 1987. In the same year she was also named the State Indian Museum's Elder of the Year. Her outstanding achievements have been recognized as well in a Riverside County proclamation and by the California state senate and assembly.

*Katherine Saubel, photographed around 1975.*

few people now know the Cahuilla language, these ceremonies (except for the religious songs) are performed in English. The few elders who still know how to perform the traditional rituals are respected and sought out for advice and assistance in social, religious, and political affairs. Young Cahuilla people respect and admire the traditional beliefs and ceremonies, and they look up to the elders who remember and practice the old ways. It is not always easy for them to develop in their lives a good blend of their own heritage and the non-Indian customs to which they are exposed daily on television, in school, and in activities on and off the reservation. Often the young people look to the elders as examples of how to maintain traditional values.

Family relationships remain very important to the Cahuillas, and some of them still use the Cahuilla terms for their relatives even though the Cahuilla language is not widely spoken anymore. However, marriages are no longer arranged by parents. Young Cahuillas now marry as they choose, sometimes to Cahuillas, often to others.

The educational process is no longer so fully centered in the family as it was before, nor do teenagers go through the traditional initiation in which clan and lineage knowledge is learned. Instead, Cahuilla children attend public schools off the reservations in local communities. An extremely important event in the lives of young people is their high school graduation. Many continue their education at local community colleges or at universities. Education is increasingly valued as opportunities for its use grow. Because the public education that Cahuilla children receive in their classes with non-Indian children does not include Cahuilla history and language, concerned Cahuillas have founded several institutions to help educate their people about their traditional way of life. Cahuilla language classes are held in some communities. Some of the elders are also working on projects to preserve their traditional culture. For instance, elder Katherine Siva Saubel has translated Cahuilla oral literature into English for presentation on National Public Radio.

The Malki Museum on the Morongo Reservation is also working to educate people about the traditional Cahuilla lifeway. It contains Cahuilla artifacts and records of Cahuilla knowledge. The Cahuilla people manage the museum and all its activities. In addition to caring for many beautiful baskets and other objects made by present and past Cahuillas, the Malki Museum also publishes books about the Cahuilla and other Indians of the area.

Every year the museum presents a fiesta on Memorial Day. At this festival, Cahuillas, other Indians, and non-Indians come to observe the holiday, celebrate their traditional culture and history, and remember Cahuilla men lost in the service of the United States during World War II, listen to traditional bird songs, eat delicious Cahuilla food, and socialize. Through events like these, Cahuillas are passing on their heritage to their young people and sharing it with outsiders.

The Cahuilla are an expanding people. Population growth is rapid, and many children are to be seen on each reservation. As urban communities extend toward the reservations, there is increased competition over the use of space. The traditional rural and small-town atmosphere of the past is giving way rapidly as Cahuilla lands are surrounded by the megalopolis of southern California. The reservations in the mountain areas are less affected than those in the San Gorgionio Pass and the desert. The urban scene has become very much a part of the milieu of young Cahuillas today, and this has important benefits. They have an improved job market and greater opportunities for education. Local community colleges offer courses near their homes, from which many go on to institutions of higher learning. Being able to keep young people close to home for the first few years after high school is important to a people who continue to maintain the close family ties that have always been a focus of Cahuilla life. Improved economic conditions have resulted from leasing Cahuilla land and developing commercial enterprises on the reservations.

Most of the traditional culture is now gone, but the remembrance of the past and respect for their culture and

*Three Cahuilla men perform bird songs at the 1983 Memorial Day fiesta. This event, held annually at the Malki Museum on Morongo Reservation, is an opportunity to celebrate the Cahuilla cultural heritage.*

history is an important factor for young as well as older Cahuillas. This is reflected in their support for publications about their culture and their concern for the preservation of cultural resources and historical archives. The Cahuilla today, entering a new era of successful economic and social adaptation, are very positive about their future. ▲

# BIBLIOGRAPHY

Barrows, David Prescott. *The Ethnobotany of the Cahuilla Indians of Southern California.* Chicago: University of Chicago Press, 1900.

Bean, Lowell John. *Mukat's People: The Cahuilla Indians of Southern California.* Berkeley: University of California Press, 1972.

Bean, Lowell John, and Katherine Siva Saubel. *Temalpakh: Cahuilla Indian Knowledge and Usage of Plants.* Banning, CA: Malki Museum Press, 1972.

Brumgardt. John R., and Larry L. Bowles. *People of the Magic Waters: The Cahuilla Indians of Palm Springs.* Palm Springs, CA: ETC Publications, 1981.

Jackson, Helen Hunt. *Ramona, A Story.* Norwood, PA: Telegraph Books, 1981. Reproduction of 1884 edition.

James, Harry C. *The Cahuilla Indians.* Banning, CA: Malki Museum Press, 1969.

Patencio, Francisco. *Stories and Legends of the Palm Springs Indians As Told to Margaret Boynton.* Los Angeles: Times-Mirror Press, 1943.

Phillips, George Harwood. *Chiefs and Challengers: Indian Resistance and Cooperation in Southern California.* Berkeley and Los Angeles: University of California Press, 1975.

Strong, William Duncan. "Aboriginal Society in Southern California." *University of California Publications in American Archaeology and Ethnology,* Vol. 26. Berkeley: University of California Press, 1929.

# THE CAHUILLA AT A GLANCE

TRIBE *Cahuilla*

CULTURE AREA *California*

GEOGRAPHY *the central part of Southern California*

LINGUISTIC FAMILY *Uto-Aztecan*

DESCENT SYSTEM *patrilineal*

RESIDENCE *patrilocal*

MAJOR FOODS *acorns, mesquite, seeds, wild fruits, antelope, mule deer, mountain sheep, small game*

ART *baskets, petroglyphs, pictographs, painted pottery, ceremonial regalia*

CURRENT POPULATION *900*

FIRST CONTACT *Juan Bautista de Anza, Spanish, 1774*

FEDERAL STATUS *recognized*

# GLOSSARY

*agent; Indian agent* A person appointed by the Bureau of Indian Affairs to supervise U.S. government programs on a reservation and/or in a specific region; after 1908 the title "superintendent" replaced "agent."

*allotment* The U.S. policy, applied nationwide through the General Allotment Act of 1887, intended to bring Indians into the mainstream by breaking up tribally owned reservations and tribal government. Each tribal member was given, or allotted, a tract of land for farming.

*anthropology* The study of the physical, social, and cultural characteristics of human beings.

*archaeology* The systematic recovery and study of evidence of human ways of life, especially that of prehistoric peoples.

*charmstone* A stone imbued with sacred powers.

*clan* A group in American Indian society that traces its descent from a common ancestor. Membership in a clan establishes membership in a tribe. Among the Cahuilla, descent and consequently clan membership are traced through the father's line only.

*ceremonial house* The building in which a Cahuilla community or clan held ceremonies and where its sacred bundle, or maiswat, was kept.

*environmental zone* A geographic area with its own characteristic animals and plants; in Cahuilla territory, there are four major environmental zones, each existing at a different altitude.

*haunik* A ritual singer who participated in ceremonies, remembered the ceremonial song cycles of an entire Cahuilla community, and helped initiate young people into adulthood.

*Indian Reorganization Act* A 1934 federal law that ended the policy of allotting plots of land to individuals and provided for political and economic development of reservation communities.

*initiation* A ritual in which boys and girls in their early teens attain the status of adults. The ritual helps them to make the transition to their new status by teaching them the social and ceremonial responsibilities of adulthood.

*?iva?a* A strong, unpredictable, and creative force, or power, that was a part of everything in the Cahuilla universe. People also possessed this force and could use it for beneficial or harmful effects.

*lineage* A line of relatives that trace their descent through the family of one's father or mother. In Cahuilla society, a lineage is the father's family, and the resulting network of relatives forms a separate community within each clan.

*Lower Sonoran Life Zone* or *desert zone* The environmental zone in Cahuilla territory that existed up to 3,500 feet above sea level; this zone had arid weather and useful plants such as cacti, palm trees, and mesquite as well as small game animals, antelope, and migratory birds.

*maiswat* A sacred bundle belonging to a Cahuilla clan; it held the supernatural power that communicated with the community's leader. It consisted of a piece of reed matting with the most sacred objects of the clan rolled up inside.

*mesquite* A spiny plant found in the southwestern United States; its seed pods were used by the Cahuilla for food.

*mission* A church, often part of a community with associated ranches and farms, formed by Spanish Catholic priests to act as a base for their efforts to help colonize California by converting the Indians to Catholicism.

*mountain life zone* The environmental zone in Cahuilla territory at 9,000 feet and more above sea level; few plants grew there, but deer, mountain sheep, and small game animals lived there in the summer.

*Mukat* One of the two original beings, according to Cahuilla mythology, and the one who became the creator, or father, of Cahuilla society and people.

*ngengewish* Ritual dancers who performed in many Cahuilla ceremonies.

*net* The religious, political, and judicial leader who was the head of each Cahuilla community.

*nukatem* The original Cahuilla beings, some of whom later would exist in the form of heavenly bodies or other natural objects.

*nukil* The most important Cahuilla ritual held every year or two to honor the dead.

*patrilineal descent* Relationships traced through the father's line.

*paxaa?* An assistant to the net who helped conduct ceremonies, solve disputes, and organize hunting parties, among other duties.

106

*pa?vu?ul* A shaman with power gained from spiritual beings, including the power to heal people and to transform himself into other creatures.

*petroglyphs* Pictures scratched or pecked into rocks with a stone.

*pictographs* Pictures painted on rocks.

*puul* A shaman with power gained from spiritual beings to cure people or to perform witchcraft.

*puvalam* The informal association of shamans that often assisted the net in decision making.

*reservation* Indian homelands either set aside by the United States or Canadian governments or retained by Indians as a result of past treaty negotiations; land designated for occupation and use by Indians. In Canada, usually called a reserve.

*shaman* A person who has special powers to call on spirit beings and mediate between the supernatural world and the world of ordinary people. Cahuilla shamans are called puul or pa?vu?ul, depending on the strength of their powers; a pa?vu?ul has more power than a puul.

*sweathouse* An airtight hut in which steam is produced by pouring water over heated rocks to help a person achieve a condition of spiritual purification.

*telmekic* The place of dead spirits.

*transition life zone* The environmental zone in Cahuilla territory at 6,300 to 9,000 feet above sea level; this zone had cool weather, rain and snow, forests and meadows, and a variety of animals such as deer, sheep, and bears.

*trust land* Land set aside and controlled by the U.S. government for use by Indians.

*Upper Sonoran Life Zone* or *high desert zone* The environmental zone in Cahuilla territory at 3,500 to 6,300 feet above sea level; the high desert zone was cooler and moister than the low desert zone and had nut-bearing trees, several fruit plants, cacti, and antelope.

# INDEX

108

# PICTURE CREDITS

LOWELL JOHN BEAN, professor of anthropology at California State University, Hayward, received his B.A., M.A., and Ph.D. in anthropology from the University of California-Los Angeles. He has worked with Cahuilla Indians since 1958. He is editor of the *Ballena Anthropology Papers* and associate editor of the *Journal of California and Great Basin Anthropology*, and has published numerous books and articles, including *Mukat's People: The Cahuilla Indians of Southern California* and *Temalpakh: Cahuilla Indian Knowledge and Usage of Plants*.

LISA J. BOURGEAULT received her B.A. from Pitzer College, Claremont, California, and has an M.A. in anthropology from the University of Arizona. She works at the Southwest Museum in Los Angeles and is interested in many Native American groups of western North America.

---

FRANK W. PORTER III, general editor of INDIANS OF NORTH AMERICA, is director of the Chelsea House Foundation for American Indian Studies. He holds a B.A., M.A., and Ph.D. from the University of Maryland. He has done extensive research concerning the Indians of Maryland and Delaware and is the author of numerous articles on their history, archaeology, geography, and ethnography. He was formerly director of the Maryland Commission on Indian Affairs and American Indian Research and Resource Institute, Gettysburg, Pennsylvania, and he has received grants from the Delaware Humanities Forum, the Maryland Committee for the Humanities, the Ford Foundation, and the National Endowment for the Humanities, among others. Dr. Porter is the author of *The Bureau of Indian Affairs* in the Chelsea House KNOW YOUR GOVERNMENT series.